T0193343

THE JOY OF THE JOURNEY
TOWARD GREATER
ENLIGHTENMENT

What My Spirit Guides Told Me

Stanley Keely, Ph.D.

BALBOA.
PRESS

A DIVISION OF HAY HOUSE

Copyright © 2018 Stanley Keely, Ph.D.

All rights reserved. No part of this book may be used or reproduced by any means, graphic, electronic, or mechanical, including photocopying, recording, taping or by any information storage retrieval system without the written permission of the author except in the case of brief quotations embodied in critical articles and reviews.

Balboa Press books may be ordered through booksellers or by contacting:

Balboa Press
A Division of Hay House
1663 Liberty Drive
Bloomington, IN 47403
www.balboapress.com
1 (877) 407-4847

Because of the dynamic nature of the Internet, any web addresses or links contained in this book may have changed since publication and may no longer be valid. The views expressed in this work are solely those of the author and do not necessarily reflect the views of the publisher, and the publisher hereby disclaims any responsibility for them.

The author of this book does not dispense medical advice or prescribe the use of any technique as a form of treatment for physical, emotional, or medical problems without the advice of a physician, either directly or indirectly. The intent of the author is only to offer information of a general nature to help you in your quest for emotional and spiritual well-being. In the event you use any of the information in this book for yourself, which is your constitutional right, the author and the publisher assume no responsibility for your actions.

Any people depicted in stock imagery provided by Getty Images are models, and such images are being used for illustrative purposes only.
Certain stock imagery © Getty Images.

Print information available on the last page.

ISBN: 978-1-9822-0232-3 (sc)
ISBN: 978-1-9822-0231-6 (hc)
ISBN: 978-1-9822-0233-0 (e)

Library of Congress Control Number: 2018904569

Balboa Press rev. date: 04/16/2018

CONTENTS

Preface...vii

Part 1

1   Introduction 1

2   Important People along My Path 4

3   Major Events in My Journey into Spirituality 6

4   Experiencing a Higher Realm 8

5   Positive Things Start to Happen Professionally.................11

6   My Evolving Views on Reality and Consciousness................ 16

Part 2

7   Communicating with My Guides 21

8   Suffering... 23

9   The Dying Process... 31

10 Creation... 33

11 We Are All One 36

12 Where Do We Go from Here? 39

13 Personal Anger... 42

14 Becoming a Better Person 45

15 What Has the Highest Priority?.............................. 48

16 Fear 50

17 Desire, Craving, Grasping 52

18 Just the Next Step 55

19 Life in the Spirit Realm 56

20 Different Levels 58

21   Self-Healing.. 60

22   Energy 63

23   Selfishness 65

Part 3

24   Where, When, and How Did My Spirit Come into Being?....... 69

25   Life Plan 71

26   Does Absolute Source (God) Think? 74

27   What Created Me?.. 78

28   Change 80

29   Beliefs I Am Unaware Of... 82

Part 4

30   A Brief Overview of My Life.................................... 87

Part 5

31   My Current Core Beliefs..113

PREFACE

I have been a seeker of spiritual knowledge for most of my life. The search for my truth (whatever that might be) has greatly intensified over the last three decades. The primary reason for this search is to gain a more in-depth understanding of existence and purpose. I was thirteen when I started to sincerely question what I heard in church, at school, and from the elders of the small, rural community I was raised in. During the last half of my life, I have been fortunate to have enough money, time, and energy to study and experience many different spiritual teachings and views. I have pursued both Western and Eastern thought. For the last ten years through the utilization of mindfulness meditation, contemplation, shamanic journeying, and what I refer to as semi-automatic writing, I believe I have been able to receive answers from the spirit realm(s) to many of my questions and concerns. Until now I have never considered writing about the information communicated to me. The primary reason I have been hesitant about describing the material I received was that I believe everyone has his or her own unique and individual spiritual path. The specific answers I received to my questions were communicated in a fashion that I could best understand at my level of consciousness. There are many more advanced individuals who might find my information sophomoric and insignificant while others may not yet be able to appreciate what I was shown. Also, I did not want to embarrass my friends and family by perhaps appearing somewhat nonsensical. I have now agreed to share my spiritual path and the insights I have received as an example of what has worked well for me. I do not think anyone should accept what I report as his or her truth; it is only mine. We are all unique and must evolve in our own particular ways. We are each responsible for our individual spiritual evolution.

I believe it is beneficial for all of us to share our spiritual views, beliefs, and opinions and to be respectful as others share theirs with us. We should open-mindedly discuss our differences and our commonalities with an attitude of accepting and allowing everyone to hold our respective positions. Because of where I now live and my physical condition, I currently have little opportunity to do that. I realize that communicating the information I have received is a one-way street. I am sharing, but there is no discussion. I regret this, but it is the best I can currently offer.

There is a short and a long answer to the question of why I am now sharing this information. The short answer and the most pertinent is that it was suggested to me by my spirit guides that I do so. The longer one is that I want to be of service to others. I am seventy-two years old. I have been a juvenile-onset, insulin-requiring diabetic since 1959 and currently have significant health challenges. With current technologies for the treatment of diabetes, it may be possible to live with the disease and have an almost normal length of life. However, very few diabetics diagnosed when I was have survived as long as I have. My guides have suggested that if I want to share their communications, I might want to start now.

When I was diagnosed with diabetes, I was a sophomore in high school and wanted to participate in sports, eat a normal teenager diet, and enjoy the excitement of adolescence. However, my weight dropped from 165 pounds to under 120 over a two- to three-month period. I was very weak and missed almost two months of school, falling well behind my classmates both scholastically and socially. While I accepted that I had to take daily insulin injections, I hated the strict low-calorie diet diabetics were given at that time, and I abhorred appearing different from my classmates, so I decided to live my life as normally as I could. I kept the fact I that I had diabetes a secret as much as possible. I ate cafeteria food (high carbohydrate), I played sports, and most importantly, I dated a few of the nicest girls in my high school. All went well. I graduated from high school and from college and was in my third year of graduate school when my diabetes, my insulin levels, and my intense exercise routine induced an extreme hypoglycemic event, allowing me to enjoy a wonderful and fascinating near-death out-of-body experience (ND/OBE). It was completely indescribable except to say it was the most significant thing that has ever happened to me. While I did not realize it at the time, my ND/OBE allowed me to briefly experience the spirit realm and started me on my spiritual quest.

In August of 2016, I developed a blister on one of my toes the would not heal. It became gangrenous and had to be amputated. Since then I have had four additional surgeries and lost two more toes. I am somewhat confined to my home (which is much better than being in a hospital) and restricted in what I can do. In an effort to be of service to others and to pursue my own path as fully as I can, I have agreed to write this book. While being somewhat talented in science and mathematics, I have never been a particularly good writer due to having ADHD and dyslexia, so attempting to develop a manuscript is something I never thought possible. But from the encouragement of people who I have shared my spiritual experiences with and help from my guides and due to the fact that (because of my physical limitations) I now have time to focus on communicating this material, I am now attempting this project. Maybe only my children will read this material. Maybe others will read it and find it beneficial. Regardless, my agreement is to write about my journey and my communications with the spirit realm.

I have been greatly blessed to have experienced this life and for the many fellow travelers who have helped me pursue my journey. I am very grateful for the guidance and help I have received from spirit. This communication is a way of expressing my gratitude to my guides and to my fellow earthly travelers for helping me learn the many lessons of this lifetime.

Love and Blessings to all,
Stan Keely, October 2017

Part 1

INTRODUCTION

I have wanted to be a spiritual explorer, writer, and teacher ever since I started investigating the spirit side of my reality. When I was young, I was extremely shy and introverted. I probably still am that way, but I love discussing nonreligious spirituality. What is contained in this book are my views, thoughts, and discoveries. They are personal to me, and they might or might not be useful to others. I believe we each have to develop and nurture our own views and revelations. While we are all in this physical adventure together, we must travel our own autonomous paths. We can and should help each other, but because we have free will, we have to make our own decisions and thereby learn the lessons we came here (to the earth) to understand. We may have developed a general life plan before we incarnated into this world, but how we actualize that plan is up to each individual. There is only one mountaintop, but there are an infinite number of paths leading to that summit. Some paths are faster or easier than others, and some of us may be more skilled climbers, but eventually we all get to the same top. I offer this material as an example of what has worked for me. Hopefully, it will help others identify ways that will catalyze their spiritual growth and evolution.

As briefly discussed in the preface, there are a number of reasons why I have now agreed to write this book. Over the past eight or nine years, I have had a number of psychics tell me I needed to consider writing a book of my thoughts on the evolution of consciousness and how I have received information on that subject from levels of higher vibration. I would guess many advertised psychics are frauds, but I also believe many are gifted individuals who can be of great benefit. I do not accept everything they communicate, but I consider it all. I also now feel my spirit guides are suggesting it is time I share some of the information they have given me. A final factor in my decision to write this book is that I currently have a major health challenge. While I hope for a significant recovery, I can think of no better way of ending this life's journey than by putting my thoughts and my guides' communications in print to be shared with anyone who might benefit from them.

My personal spiritual views are not static but very dynamic, constantly changing and evolving. It appears that my ability to interact with the spirit realm has grown as I have become more open to receiving answers from that source. I am not implying I have any kind of special ability or talent. I am certain that my current views and beliefs are far from being absolutely correct. I am equally certain that as my consciousness continues to evolve, my understanding will expand and my views will change. My views today are much superior to my views from five, ten, twenty, or sixty years ago.

During the 1990s, I undertook a study of each of the seven largest world religions in an attempt to see what they had in common. I thought if I could find commonalities between them, those attributes might represent deep relative truths I could apply to my life. I found several concepts that were shared between all or most of these belief systems. While I respect and honor all sincere spiritual teachings, I find that formal religion often creates a division rather than a unity. As long as members of a religion think theirs is the only true and correct view or belief, I tend to avoid being involved with them. From all that I have learned, I believe I have found the way that works best for me at this time and that gives me answers to my search in the form I can understand.

There is a Taoist view that one cannot obtain enlightenment if one is searching for it. I accept this view. When something is ready, it will happen. But I have been trained as a research scientist and by nature am interested in how and why things come into and go out of existence and how I might personally affect those processes. My personal path has to start with an intellectual understanding that identifies my current best guess—the best that I have at this time. I realize eventually I will need to cease my attempts to experience things through my brain and allow my answers to self-manifest. I may be at an early stage in my awakening, but I thoroughly enjoy the process.

2

IMPORTANT PEOPLE ALONG MY PATH

I refer to my personal philosophy as Stanism (Stan is my name, and the *ism* is to indicate it is my personal view). It changes regularly as my awareness and understanding increase. As I became more aware of my life's path, my experiences, and the lessons I have learned, my philosophy formed, grew, and evolved. Every person who touched my life had some effect on its expansion. I would like to especially thank nine wonderful people who agreed to walk major portions of my life path with me. At various times we gave each other love, anger, joy, pain, kindness, judgment, caring, jealousy, and support. In doing so they allowed or caused me to experience the many invaluable lessons that have supported my spiritual evolution. I am sure they have benefited equally from my being in their lives. From a spiritual perspective, everyone we devote significant time and energy to helps us grow, including those individuals we consider our enemies. The nine saints who make up my inner circle of earthly travelers in this lifetime are my father, Stan (who moved on thirty years ago); my mother, Eva, who l will say a bit more about below; my brother, Mike; my two children, Kristen and Robert; my first wife, Corrine; my second wife, Linda; my soul mate, Debra; and my partner, Tisa. I am extremely grateful for having each of these people play the roles they have in my life, and I love them all very much.

My very Christian mother played a paramount role in the development of my secular philosophy. She usually has very firm views about most things and does not back down from a good discussion (i.e., argument). I have been told I share this characteristic with her; however, my views are somewhat fluid and regularly change. Until recently, whenever I visited her we would spend the last few hours of my stay with a lively discussion of our differing views of reality. I modified my views with each discussion, although hers did not change, for which I am very happy. She draws great joy and comfort from her belief system, and I would not want that to change. As our discussions would become more heated, I would often hear myself express some rather profound and insightful views I had not considered before. Often as I drove back to whatever state I was living in at the time, I would reflect on what I had said. I was always surprised at how much sense it made to me. I would then modify my Stanist philosophy to include these new thoughts, views, and ideas. I do not know where my new thoughts came from (internal or external) but am grateful to my mother for being so argumentative.

My mother and I love each other very much, but we are polar opposites. This brings the heat to our fiery discussions. The other eight members of my spiritual posse played different but equally important roles in my life (often more pleasant) and in my development of Stanism. One of them even came up with the term Stanism. Their roles were usually supportive, but at times they provided critical and opposing views to my thinking. I go into some detail about each of these loved ones in part 4 of this book. I hold great love and respect toward each of my nine major human teachers. I am sure we all knew what we were getting into before incarnating into our present lives, and I am completely grateful we played the roles we did.

3

MAJOR EVENTS IN MY JOURNEY
INTO SPIRITUALITY

A few years ago, I read an article written by a secular humanist that began by stating, "There is no God, there is no life after death, there is nothing beyond the physical." I personally do not like to use the term *God*, as it often carries different preconceived ideas for different groups. I might agree with the secularist if he were referring to one of the Greek or Roman gods or one of the gods presented as the "one and only true god," as is usually done by most religious movements. For the sake of full disclosure (or near full), I do believe that all that is came from somewhere or something outside normal space-time, or at least got started from that source—the so-called uncaused cause. I prefer using terms such as Source, Absolute, or Creator. It is the reason there is something and not nothing. Currently, my preferred term is Absolute Source. I do not use "the" Source, since that may cause it to appear to be something that is separate, rather than being all prevailing. I believe Absolute Source is beyond our human ability to comprehend or understand. That belief does not keep me from trying to experience Source as best I can and to understand the various worlds or realms we exist in. I most certainly believe there is more to existence than just the physical and that our essence(s) or consciousness continues after the death of the physical body. Absolute Source is nondualistic, and therefore I do not believe in the existence of a classic heaven and hell. Nor do I believe in divine punishment. I feel that evil does exist but that it is of human creation and not a holy-evil cosmic duality. I do believe in karma (i.e., cause and effect), but not in good and bad. Many times I feel something is bad only to later realize it was very beneficial (i.e., me developing diabetes). I usually do not believe in anything that invokes dualism (up/down, light/dark, low/high). These things are necessary for comparison and to keep score but are not of an absolute everlasting nature. Obviously, there are many awful, inhuman things in our world that we all should do everything we can to stop or prevent (the Crusades, the Holocaust, slavery, genocide, terrorism, racism, violence, etc.). Hopefully as we evolve spiritually, we will realize we are all one and stop inflicting so much suffering on others and ourselves.

4

EXPERIENCING A HIGHER REALM

The major reason I so strongly believe in an afterlife and the existence of higher non-physical realms is the near-death experience (NDE) I had in 1968. In the fall of that year, I was a graduate student at Kent State University in Kent, Ohio. I was married to my first wife, Corrine, who was a nurse. I had been diagnosed with type 1 insulin-dependent diabetes in 1959, and when I moved from Pennsylvania to Ohio to study for my doctorate (1966), I started seeing a new local physician. My new doctor immediately changed the type of insulin I was taking from PZI insulin (very long acting) to Lente insulin (shorter duration of activity). This was well before diabetics started to measure their blood glucose levels directly, and they were then dependent on a relatively imprecise urine analysis to get a crude blood glucose level estimate. Shortly after being diagnosed, I had observed that exercise helped me control my diabetes and allowed me to eat more, so I became an avid exerciser. That fall I had joined a graduate school intramural basketball league that played on Tuesday evenings. One night after a particularly long and strenuous game, I came home exhausted and only ate a piece of toast before going to bed rather than the cheeseburger and two beers that was my usual bedtime snack. This was a perfect storm for a hypoglycemic event, which did occur. It drove me into a physically unconscious state. I became aware of my consciousness floating above my physical body, which laid motionless in deep coma on the bed below. I felt absolutely no attachment to that body but did realize what had happened to it (strenuous activity and less-than-the-normal carbohydrate ingestion). I remember thinking, *That poor dumb man. He really messed up.* Words cannot describe what I experienced next, but I will do my best to portray it. My attention or awareness went to a huge, extremely bright cloud of golden-white light that at first moved toward me and then engulfed me in its warm, brilliant presence. I realize that golden-white light does not exist, but that is what best describes what I experienced. It was not a mixture or shade. It was different from anything I had ever experienced. It was pure and singular. I felt completely at home, as if this were the place I was always meant to be.

I had been raised a fundamentalist Christian and thought it might be Jesus or God. I had left my earlier beliefs and was somewhat a new ager and thought the light might be my higher self. I still have no idea what it was, but it was completely accepting, without any judgment, and radiated what I will call unconditional love. The only words that come to mind to describe how I felt are: complete bliss, unmatched joy, absolute belonging, and pure love. These are just words trying to describe an experience that was indescribable.

While I was engulfed in the cloud of light, I noticed my wife standing in the corner of our bedroom and saw my doctor standing over my body. My wife had realized something was wrong when our alarm did not rouse me. When I did not respond to her attempts to wake me, she called my doctor at his home. I observed my doctor try to inject a huge syringe of something into a vein in my right hand. I was later informed that he injected two fifty-cc syringes of glucose into a hand vein since most of the big veins in my arms had collapsed. I then noticed two men, who today would be referred to as EMTs, standing in the bedroom doorway holding a stretcher. While I was out of body, I could tell what my wife and doctor were thinking, although there was little or no communication between them.

My doctor, who was now sitting on the bed, still holding the now empty second fifty-cc syringe, looked up at the EMTs, and said, "I think he is going to make it. We may not need you, but stick around awhile." Then the golden-white cloud of light started to recede, and I faded back into my body and regained physical consciousness. My NDE was over, and I experienced very significant depression being back in a material body. I do not remember being given a choice to return to my body or to go on. Being out of body was so wonderful that I do not believe I would have made the choice to return. Maybe I do not remember making the choice or maybe some other energy decided for me. My depression (disappointment) dissolved over the next few weeks, and within a month I was back to my normal physical existence. I did not know how to process my experience and told no one about it for many years. About ten years after my NDE, I learned about the work of Dr. Raymond Moody on NDEs. Then I realized that that was what I had experienced. While I do not remember a dark tunnel, meeting loved ones who had already passed over, or a life review, my experience was not too different from most other NDEs: wonderful bright light and feelings of belonging, bliss, joy, peace, and love. I had the realization that we are far more than our physical bodies and that a spiritual realm(s) exists.

I wish I could definitely say that my experience immediately gave me great insight, dramatically changed my life, or made me a better person, but I cannot. It may have produced those effects and I did not realize it or they may have occurred gradually and I did not notice. I am not sure. I was still filled with fear and anger and had low self-esteem. I continued to have difficulties with relationships. But I had a newfound peace about death and a greatly increased interest in nonphysical existence.

Several months after my NDE, my wife and I separated and were in the process of getting a divorce when she was tragically killed in an early-morning auto accident in February 1970. At the moment of her death (2:43 a.m.) I awoke with a heavy feeling of loss and sadness. I feel she reached out to tell me she was transitioning out of her physical life.

5

Positive Things Start to Happen Professionally

By my early teens, I had stopped accepting things just because most people said or believed they were so. I started searching for my own truth. That search appears to have accelerated shortly after my NDE, although it was not obvious to me at the time. By the mid '80s, my search had become one of the primary focuses of my life and has brought me to my current level of understanding. I could easily believe that a seed was planted during my NDE that eventually drove me to become the spiritual explorer I feel I am today.

Many people say that earthly life is like a school and that all the things that happen during our lifetime are opportunities to learn lessons and/or make discoveries. I am not sure I completely accept that view, but I do not reject it. I have had five major committed relationships in my life with four beautiful, loving, and intelligent women. (Yes, one of those wonderful beings decided to give me a second shot.) The first four relationships ended in what I originally thought was failure. Viewed with the benefit of time, I now appreciate that I learned and experienced much from the beginning, duration, and ending of those relationships. I am very grateful that those wonderful ladies were part of my life. I am still good friends with the surviving three. All four allowed me to learn some painful but important lessons, and in that sense, our relationships were very successful. If, as I choose to believe, we are born into the physical world with some sort of life plan, then I would say our coming together and coming apart were all part of my school's curriculum.

As I will next review, I have had six major jobs. I was hired into each one, learned from each position and environment, and then moved on to a new position that required me to face new obstacles and evolve both personally and professionally. I had originally intended to work my entire life for a single company, as my father had done. Looking back, I realize how difficult it was changing jobs so often and having to prove myself again with each new position, but I also see how much each change allowed or caused me to grow and expand my abilities. I am grateful to all my previous bosses, even though we often saw things very differently.

After the death of my wife in 1970, I was filled with regret and guilt. I had little motivation or focus. After several weeks, I returned to my laboratory and finished the last few experiments I needed to complete my PhD research. I had just started writing my dissertation when May 4, 1970, happened, where four Kent State students were shot and killed by the Ohio National Guard and several others were badly wounded. Occurring so close to my first wife's death, these killings had a huge impact on me. I learned how suddenly and unexpectedly physical death can come.

Until I took my first philosophy class during my sophomore year in college, I believed many of the Christian teachings I had heard from various preachers, teachers, and community elders. By the spring of 1970, those teachings and my childhood faith stopped making much sense. I started searching in earnest for a religion or spiritual path that would comfort me and help me better understand life. As my spiritual search expanded, I started questioning everything I heard, saw, or read. I accepted nothing unless it was logical and could withstand debate. I did not realize it, but my spiritual journey had begun, and it would lead me in an entirely new direction. I am very grateful for my early training in Christianity because it exposed me to the teachings of Jesus on love, peace, forgiveness, joy, nonjudgement, and service. These are teachings that many people who say they know Christ as their personal savior appear never to have learned with their willingness to destroy anybody or anything that does not align with their views and beliefs. This attitude is, of course, common to most religions. I often wonder why the beautiful teachings of Jesus on love, compassion, caring, and service are commingled in a book (i.e., the Bible) filled with stories of violence, hatred, and inhumane behavior.

After finishing my PhD at Kent State, I did two years of postdoctoral research at Ohio State University. This is where I met my second wife, Linda. I had become dissatisfied with the type of research I had been doing (organic chemistry) and wanted to change my focus to biochemistry and molecular biology. I learned that a professor at Vanderbilt University had just won the Nobel Prize in Medicine and Physiology and decided to see if I might be able to attend Vanderbilt and study for a second PhD working with that Nobel Laureate. I was invited to interview at Vandy and was very happily surprised when the Department of Physiology (which had a heavy focus on medical biochemistry) offered me a visiting investigator position rather than a graduate student fellowship. This position paid me a lot more money and allowed me to just do research with no additional course work requirements. So my new wife and I loaded a U-Haul and headed to Nashville.

Even though I felt intellectually inferior to most of the other staff members, I worked very hard and my research went surprisingly well. (Two decades later I was diagnosed with ADHD, which has a low self-esteem characteristic associated with it.) I was able to publish several scientific papers on my work and was awarded a small research grant that allowed me to hire support staff to assist me. Even before I moved to Nashville, I had visualized/fantasized about becoming a full-time tenure-track faculty member at a high-powered school like Vanderbilt but still was surprised when such a position was later offered to me. Originally, I had been uncertain if I was intelligent enough to graduate from college. Now I had not only graduated with honors but had earned a doctorate and was a faculty member at a very prestigious university in a beautiful and exciting city. While, because of my ADHD-induced poor self-image, I was constantly afraid people would realize I really did not know much, I very much enjoyed academic life.

For the first half of the '70s, I spent my time doing research, publishing my results, getting research grants, and partying. For a person who had not had his first sip of beer until his second year of graduate school (1967), I quickly made up for the lost time and developed the reputation as a person who enjoyed "bending the elbow" and socializing. My first child (daughter Kristen) was born in the summer of 1976. Although I felt unprepared to become a father, I really enjoyed our little girl. Once she became mobile, I started going home from the lab early so the two of us could play before her bedtime. I started to resent not spending more time with my new family because of the "publish or perish" demands of my work.

In the mid-'70s, I also started a crude meditation and visualization practice. At that time, I did not realize that I had been using visualization, which for me is similar to imagination, to manifest various situations in my life, including my academic appointment. As a child, I had been demeaned for daydreaming much of the time. Upon reflection, I eventually understood that I had drawn many physical objects, interactions, and experiences into my life by first visualizing them in my mind.

Although I was shy and hated public speaking, researchers and faculty members are usually required to publicly present their work. Once successful, they are often invited to lecture at other universities and at scientific meetings. I found that if I spent an hour visualizing the result I desired from a public talk, I usually got that result. Often I could see specific questions that I would be asked after my presentations while doing my pretalk visualizations. Most of my colleagues thought I was a naturally confident speaker who enjoyed being in front of an audience. At the time that was far from the truth. With my success, I eventually learned to trust my intuition and visualization prowess and became somewhat relaxed speaking even to large groups.

I now view visualization as using the power of thought to create or help create a desired result. If I use it to affect my personal performance, it often works. Obviously, it is not as successful when several people or groups want conflicting outcomes. Visualization, which I now believe is thought form generation, and meditation are now cornerstones of my spiritual practices.

In an effort to have more time with my family, I resigned my academic appointment in 1979 and accepted a position as a senior scientist with a major pharmaceutical company—an offer I helped generate through the power of visualization.

6

My Evolving Views on Reality and Consciousness

After leaving Vanderbilt, my professional career continued to go well. I changed companies several times over the next twenty years, with each new position bringing a higher level of responsibility, more authority, and more remuneration. However, I seemed to become less and less content.

The birth of my second child (son Robert) in 1983 brought me great personal joy and happiness. Even as an infant he was (and still is) a calm, caring, kind being. While it is difficult to tell how advanced an incarnated spirit is, I expect both of my children are way ahead of me. They are both very intelligent and possess a deep desire to help others. I greatly admire them both and use them as personal examples as I try to become a better person. Both are involved in the healing arts and are of great service to their communities and the world.

Despite having an idyllic family, the relationship between me and my wife was becoming strained, and we functioned more and more independently and rarely did things together. We would eventually separate and then divorce.

Professionally I was now completely out of the research lab and into higher levels of management. While I was still very shy and did not like addressing problems or engaging in conflict, I found I had good people skills, vision, and foresight. This was at least in part due to me having a great deal of empathy, and I often could read how a person felt or how he or she was responding to what was being said. I was also good at reading (and sending) body language (energy). My parents had taught me to be honest, caring, fair, and giving. That coupled with my ability to read people and to effectively create through visualization allow me to manifest a work environment where my group, section, or department could succeed. The areas I managed usually outperformed most others.

As I grew more aware of the benefits of having a safe and fair work environment, I also became aware of the importance of the mental, emotional, and spiritual aspects in developing the success environment I wanted. This awareness coupled with the help and encouragement of a very important person who had come into my life (my soul mate?, Debra) drove me to explore the extra dimensions of existence. I was particularly drawn to the work of Dr. Stanislav Grof on nonordinary states of consciousness. I read hundreds of books and attended almost one hundred seminars and workshops on consciousness, the evolution of consciousness, the use of thought in manifesting, etc. While I maintained my well-paying executive day job, with the help of my special person, I founded a free after-work activity/service called Total Life Development. This was an effort to help people balance the physical, mental, and spiritual aspects of their lives (body/mind/spirit). While my soul mate (?) and I eventually went our separate ways (the reason for the ?), she greatly helped me move onto a new and very special spiritual path.

In the fall of 2000, I started working with a holistic coach (similar to a life coach) to help me deal with an accumulation of personal losses. My normal way of handling loss was to internalize it and continue to function as best I could. After years of doing this, it was taking a severe toll on my health. I benefit very much from my one-on-one sessions with this coach and accepted an invitation to begin a series of eleven workshops that would allow me to become a certified holistic coach myself. At the third workshop of this series, I met a very dynamic lady (partner Tisa) who was very spiritual but nonreligious. She had a wonderful sense of humor, and we quickly become friends, then life partners, and then business partners. Because of my professional success and ten years of corporate stock options,

I was able to retire in 2002 at the age of fifty-seven. Our partnerships (both personal and business) lasted only a few years, but during that time, we were able to travel widely studying comparative religion, Buddhism, Shamanism, cranial sacral therapy, heart-centered therapy, and clinical hypnosis. Buddhist mindfulness meditation and shamanic journeying are two of the four cornerstones of my current spiritual practice. Because of what I experienced during that quest, I developed my personal spiritual philosophy, which I now refer to as Stanism. After we came apart, my now ex-partner and I both continued our personal spiritual quests.

In 2009 my soul mate and I reconnected and started seeing each other as time and distance allowed. In May 2011, I moved from central Ohio into a beautiful rural sanctuary-like home in central Tennessee. (See the latter sections of part 4 in this book for how things magically fell in place to allow this move.) Both my children and my soul mate from the 1990s currently live within ten to forty miles of me and my retreat-like home. I benefit greatly from having these three loved ones so close. I also have significant alone time to study, contemplate, meditate, and communicate with the spirit realm. Health issues currently prevent me from interacting with my family as much as I would like, and I have given up most physical activities (golf, gym work, going out, etc.).

Hopefully this is only temporary. It does give more time to deepen my spiritual practices. Currently my typical day is to rise early and read some type of scientific (astrology, quantum mechanics etc.), metaphysic, or consciousness literature. I then go into my shrine room and meditate and contemplate for a set period. This is followed by a shamanic journey to obtain information on a particular subject from the spirit realm. Immediately after my journey, I do a form of semiautomatic writing to document whatever information I have received. I believe the information I receive during my morning spiritual sessions is a gift to me from higher vibrational levels. I share some of these communications in part 2 of this book. They may or may not resonate with you. Remember, as I stressed earlier, we all have our own individual path to follow and grow by. Paraphrasing what the Buddha said, this is what I have learned. Accept from it that which works for you and discard the rest.

Part 2

7

COMMUNICATING WITH MY GUIDES

I will now share some of the information I believe I have received from higher nonphysical sources. The information received was usually in response to a specific question or concern I was pondering.

As discussed earlier, my procedure for receiving information usually begins in the morning with a strong pot of coffee while, in an effort to expose myself to new or different views, I read some type of spiritual material. Then I meditate for a set period. My questions usually start to be formulated during this period even though I attempt to focus only on the object of my meditation (i.e., the breath). I then do a period of contemplative meditation where I often begin receiving information. Next, I go on a shamanic journey where the bulk of the information is transmitted. Finally, I write down what I have received. I never filtered or edited the material. Almost always additional information will flow through me as I write.

Occasionally I attempt to contact a specific spirit during my shamanic journey. Often it is the revered Shambhala Buddhist teacher Chogyam Trungpa Rinpoche, who I have connected with after his death by studying his teachings and by going on long (four-week) meditation and study retreats. Also over the last two years I have been visited by an energy that appears in my mind as the image I hold for Jesus Christ.

My contact with the Christ came about in a surprising way. I had been studying some teachings that stressed the benefit of following a master teacher or avatar. I was unaware of any specific living master and realized it would probably be difficult for me to interact with one if there was one on the physical plane. So I decided to attempt interacting with an ascended master. I asked that one such ascendant master appear to me and did a meditation/contemplation session to see if such an energy would reveal itself. Since I had been very involved with Buddhism, I expected to be visited by some high-ranking Bodhisattva. Much to my surprise, Jesus came to me. I had often used his name as a profanity and though his appearance was unusual, although I did not fear being judged or reprimanded. He/she/it smiled and said, "Bet you didn't expect to get me." He then pointed out that all true masters project from the same energy—an energy of love and peace and joy. No judgment, no right or wrong, just the desire to be of help to those trying to grow spiritually. She/he/it said it appeared to me in the form *it* did because I had been overly critical of the Christian hierarchies and I needed to be more allowing and less judgmental toward all people. It said it appeared as the Christ image to "press my buttons." I have received much beneficial guidance from this energy of Jesus. It has great insight and presents information in a way I can comprehend. It also exhibits a wonderful sense of humor.

8

Suffering

Question: Why is there so much suffering in the world?

This is a question I had struggled with for some time. I wondered if the *creator (god)* was kind, caring, and loving (as I would like to believe) or uninvolved, or worse, malevolent. Why would a caring, loving Creator allow people, animals, and even the planet to suffer as much as they appear to? And why is that universal suffering so disproportionate? While no one can tell what another person is feeling or experiencing, most people like me (white, lower middle/middle class, children of the '50s and '60s, born into a developed country) have adequate food, water, and shelter while the urban poor and people in less developed countries or in areas where war is raging do not have enough of any of these.

When I was young and raised this question, I was told by the church elders that we were blessed by god and should be grateful. They seemed to be saying it was a matter of luck. Even at twelve or thirteen this did not make sense to me. My initial response was anger with the Creator, thinking it must be an uncaring or uninvolved force. After much meditation and contemplation along with reflection on the love and peace I felt during my near-death out of body experience, I realized that a wonderful spiritual existence awaits after we rid ourselves of the physical body and reasoned that something had created a very accepting and loving realm. I now consider the universe, if we include the nonphysical realm(s), to be a wonderful, beautiful home.

Some people say that suffering is necessary because it creates contrasts, which allow or give us the opportunities to learn various lessons. They usually add that an earthly existence is difficult but it allows a more rapid development. I can somewhat accept this, but again the disproportionality causes me major problems. I do believe in reincarnation and in karma, but still I am not convinced that this is the reason some people suffer much more than others. (Please note: To me karma is not a form of reward/ punishment. It is just the universal principle that we get back what we give out—the golden rule and all that stuff.)

After being conflicted by this question most of my adult life, I ask my spirit friends to give me some understanding. Their response was in the form of a "what if" question. The information was given to me during several journeys over a three-month period. I need to again stress that this was given in a way I could best understand. Physical existence is far too complex for me to understand it in the absolute. I was assured that the answer I received was correct at a certain level, a level I could understand, but it was not the entire explanation.

Normally I will present the information as my Guides communicated it to me and use the personal pronoun "you". At other times, I will use "I" to help flow and clarity.

Here is a summary of those communications.

Guide's response (in question form): What if Creator/Source/God is a growing, expanding, evolving principle?

Obviously Absolute Source is ultimately responsible for and is everything that is. It may not, however, be everything that will ever be. Perhaps *it* is not static but is dynamically growing and evolving. It is open and can expand, not static or closed. At the present time, you (all human beings) are the vanguard for this evolution/expansion in the physical earthly realm. Since you and everything else are part of Source, as your consciousness evolves and as you create, Source then too evolves and grows as the expanding creations are added to everything that is. The human species is the most advanced species on earth and so has the greatest impact on this evolution.

You use your intellect, imagination, intuition, and circumstance to direct this growth. You try something either physically, politically, spiritually, or culturally, and if it works, you adopt it. If it does not, you throw it out and try something new. That makes you (humans) responsible for the situations you find yourselves in today, both the good and the not so good. You have free will, so you decide the directions you individually and collectively move in. In part, you are the implementers for the evolution of Source/Creator. If you determined your direction from a center of love, sharing, mutual support, and kindness, you will grow and prosper. If you make poor decisions based on greed, anger, hatred, fear, and selfishness, you will destroy yourself as well as much of all life on earth.

If this were to happen, Source would simply use the next species that evolves into the "top dog" role to grow through. Your particular individual spirits, after additional learning and realization in the non-physical realms, might become part of that new species. Let's hope you can start making better decisions before you destroy yourselves. Good luck.

Of course, all this could be my imagination, but it is what I was given to consider, and it does explain to me why, despite the Creator being the source of all love, the world experiences so much suffering. We have free will to create and have made many wonderful advancements. We have also made many mistakes that have led us to the brink of destruction. It is time we move past our selfishness, greed, and need to dominate and start making decisions from a center of love, caring, compassion, and wisdom.

Follow-Up Question 1: *Why do we humans make such poor decisions and thereby create suffering?*

It is an oversimplification, but it might be more easily understood by examining the current level of physical evolution of the human race. With the development of higher brain function (formation/development of the prefrontal lobe), animals/humans started to develop the capacity to make decisions that can benefit others as well as self—a more altruistic approach based on reason, reflection, understanding, awareness, kindness, caring, and selflessness.

Prior to this, decisions were based on more animalistic instincts (the reptilian brain), which were characterized by self-preservation, dominance, selfishness, fear, and violence. As human consciousness developed, people began to realize that behaviors that harm others will eventually harm them as well. The ability to observe, reflect, and reason leads to an understanding of what behaviors are helpful as compared to those that are more self-destructive. The human species is in the process of evolving from the animal kingdom into the human kingdom. Some individuals are further along that evolutionary path than others. The ones most evolved might be called humanitarians while the least evolved might be called thieves, murders, fear mongers, dictators, and terrorists. Unfortunately, many of the current world leaders would not be considered humanitarians but rather selfish, power-hungry tyrants. In much of the developed world, these people are elected into positions of power. As long as the majority of the citizenry vote for this type of person, suffering will continual. Consciousness evolution progresses along a bell-shaped curve. As more and more people move their decision-making activities into their prefrontal cortexes, they will select better leaders. It currently is undetermined how fast or if the human species will evolve.

Follow-Up Question 2: *What can we do to ease suffering?*

I will share some of the things that were suggested as ways we could help ease suffering first as individuals and then as part of the collective.

Individually
It has been often pointed out that all humans experience pain, but you can choose whether to suffer or not. (Originally, I was not sure what this meant or how it might help relieve suffering. After much meditation, contemplation, and journeying, I was shown the following.)

All normally functional sentient beings experience pain: acute or chronic, physical, emotional, or spiritual. That is part of having a physical body with its pain receptors, nerves, and brain. Most of the time the pain is short lived and eventually recedes. If you mentally attach and personally identify with that pain, you empower it, and it will stay with you much longer. You suffer, in part, because you believe the pain is part of you rather than something you are experiencing at that time. Getting angry at the object you think is responsible for the pain (person, situation, deity, etc.) will help change it into suffering, and you will carry it with you until you decide to let it go or to numb yourselves to it through suppression, pain pills, alcohol, drugs, etc.

Forgiveness is necessary to completely remove suffering, whether it is toward the chair that you bumped into, the lover who left you, the deity who took your loved one away or caused/allowed you to be born into a difficult environment. You should not ignore physical pain, but realizing that it is there and it will go away allows that pain to dissipate more quickly.

I was also shown that while people need to be aware of what is happening around them and should try to reduce pain and suffering as much as they reasonably can, they should not personally identify with their pain or the pain of others. Nor should they believe the pain is part of themselves or others.

(This guidance was very important for me. I am a very empathic person and often am able to feel the energy of people around me. As a compassionate human being, I try to help people who suffer, but I now am careful not to take on their feelings. If I feel someone is frightened, I will try to help them to feel safe and to become comfortable. I now am careful not to personally experience their fear myself as I could easily do.)

Another helpful suggestion was: "Attempt to see what might be good in a situation or experience versus always looking for what might be wrong with it. Humans often see something as being very wrong, only to later realize it was actually beneficial." I was also shown that there is a lesson or opportunity in everything, but I am not evolved enough to completely integrate that view into my mind-set.

A few days later, I was shown that by being of service to others, I would reduce my individual suffering. Many people find when they put their pain aside and help other people, their pain is reduced or completely vanishes. I know several people who, despite being ill, serve meals or give other service to the homeless during Thanksgiving and Christmas. While they are doing this, they usually feel much better. Lending help to those less fortunate than ourselves helps them and helps us.

My guides showed me that while I should try to always be aware and available that I should avoid the pain of guilt when I do not take advantage of an apparent opportunity to help. As I said earlier, I am a very empathetic person. This often gives me some insight into what other people are feeling. It also can produce guilt and pain when I do not come to their aid if they seem to be in need. I was shown that sometimes it is better to leave people alone so they can resolve their own issues. Other times it is better to give help. It was communicated that being compassionate, caring, and of service does not always mean I need to be or should become involved. I was advised to stay open and aware of my internal guidance (intuition) and to respond as I was led. I may not really be missing an opportunity but rather allowing the individual the space he or she needs to find his or her way and through his or her own efforts, grow.

One time a couple of Buddhist friends and I were having a decision about suffering and karma. Some people who do not understand the principle of karma believe what happens to a person is because of his or her misdeeds. I stated that sometimes other people's apparent misfortune is actually an opportunity for us to be of service. There was some agreement about this, and then a very well-practiced Buddhist added, "Regardless of whether a person is in need do to their karma or not, it is our karma to help them." I found this to be quite insightful.

Several years ago, my guides/teachers showed me a somewhat metaphysical way I could help reduce the suffering of others by sending "LoveLight" to them. This is something I was introduced to during my readings about light workers and my own ND/OBE, where I was embraced by what seemed to me as a golden-white cloud of light that felt like something I would call unconditional love.

Since, due to illness, I am currently somewhat uninvolved with the outside world and am not able to be of direct service to others, now as part of my meditation practice, I often mentally visualize drawing down what I call golden-white LoveLight from a higher vibrational level and directing it to people I know are in need. I hope this is of service to those individuals. Although I do not get the good feeling of directly experiencing my acts of service, this may actually be better since LoveLight can go where it can best be used rather than me doing something that I think will be helpful. I believe LoveLight can also be sent to areas of the world where large groups of people are suffering from natural disasters, war, poverty, and cruelty. My individual practice can be viewed as my way of praying for others.

Globally

Guide's response: As discussed earlier, the human species is responsible for some, most, or all of the suffering in the world. You need to take responsibility for reducing it by making better decisions as individuals and as groups. The world is full of fear, hatred, selfishness, and intolerance. You need do all you can to rid yourselves of these life-reducing emotions and to help others do the same. You can change the world, and while it has to start by changing your individual selves, you can (must) support and perhaps become involved with programs to feed the hungry, give aid to the sick, help the environment, and change the short-sighted, power-seeking politicians in power now into public servants with wisdom and compassion for all people. There are numerous wonderful organizations that you can donate to, volunteer to, or do whatever you can to compassionately bring about better decision making and positive change.

Follow-Up Question 3: *What is the most important thing for me to do?*

I am currently seventy-two years old and have several health issues. Given my current situation, what is the most important/beneficial thing I can do to help both myself and others to evolve spiritually?

Communication from my guides: You need to have faith and confidence in yourself and in your internal wisdom. When you still yourself for a moment, you will know the best thing to say and/or do when a situation or opportunity presents itself. Your contribution will have a greater positive impact if you remember we are all one, from the same Absolute Source, and remove any selfish thoughts your ego might generate. Make full use of your kindness, compassion, intellect, and most importantly, intuition. Do not allow animalistic instinct to affect your actions.

9

THE DYING PROCESS

One of the results of my near-death experience is that I have little or no fear about death, but still I am not too comfortable with the process of dying. I hope to have a quick, peaceful, and painless death. Being relatively healthy and happy, going to sleep, and waking up in LoveLight—no pain, no fuss, no mess. However, many spiritual traditions believe that the time of death is an opportunity for significant spiritual growth. Being aware as death approaches can be beneficial to the dying person and perhaps to those around him or her. This is not to suggest that pain medication should not be used. Being as comfortable as possible is very important for the dying person. Having some idea as to what to expect as the dying process advances allows the person to be mentally and spiritually involved in that process. Even if the individual is comatose, the consciousness is fully functional.

Question: What can I do to make my dying process easy but also be an event that supports maximum evolution of my consciousness?

Communication from guides and an ancestor: During my normal shamanic journey, a distant relative appeared in my mind's eye. He had been killed in some European battle around 1750. He said he was initially surprised to realize the dead on both sides of the battle were traveling together into the light (LoveLight?) with no anger, hatred, or fear. Then he gave me some important specific directions. He said that the most important thing to remember during the dying process was to be excited because you are going on the most beautiful, wonderful trip you could imagine. *(Like the song says, "Don't worry, be happy"—my words not his.)*

The second thing he suggested was to forgive everybody and everything. If I could not completely forgive all, I was to do the best I could. The less fear one has (the more excited) and the more forgiving, the better and easier the transition will be.

I have had the great good fortune to share these thoughts with people during the last days of their earthly lives, and it appears to work as reported by the dying person and/or his or her family.

While speaking with people in their dying process, they have often told me that they see and talk with loved ones who are already in spirit. These visitations seem to bring great comfort to the dying person. Some appear to enjoy talking to living loved ones about their experiences. People sometimes think they are imaging these visits (which could be true, but my guides have shown me they are very real) and are comforted when others accept their experiences. I have also been shown that it helps if loved ones assure the dying person that it is completely appropriate for them to share what they are experiencing as they approach transition.

10

CREATION

From an early age, I have been interested in cosmology and the creation of the physical universe. When I was young, I would look up at the star-filled night sky and wonder what it might have been like 13 to 14 billion years before. How did things progress to take us from nothing or almost nothing to where we can now formulate reasonable theories about what may have transpired to get us here as well as to design scientific experiments to test those theories? I also wondered how life came about. Was there a specific driver to cause life to arise and evolve as it has, or was it all due to time and random mutation? As discussed earlier, I was shown a message that we are responsible for our own evolution and that we evolve through our trial and error activities. Since the development of the "Big Brain" (i.e., prefrontal cortex, coupled with our increasing ability to observe, reason, and reflect), we should now be able to move beyond the "try it and see if it works" era into a stage where the likelihood of success is greater.

Question: How, when, and where did creation get started?

During a contemplation and journey on the formation of the early universe, I was given the following pictures and narrative on how things developed. Everything I received was very anthropomorphized, probably so I could better understand what my guides were trying to communicate. I am human and can best relate to things and events if they are given some rudimentary human characteristics. I take no issue if you think the concept of primordial wisdom is pure craziness, but it is what I was shown and the idea resonates with me. What follows is a description of what I was shown. I did not receive advice but rather a lengthy series of picture communications.

The basic concept I was shown is that everything in physical existence has associated with it some amount of what was labeled primordial wisdom. Also present is a basic drive to create (perhaps by the trial and error method described earlier—my thought). Looking back in time to shortly after the big bang, one of the first things to arise from the coalescence of energies were subatomic particles such as quarks, along with others. Two of these quarks decided to join together to see what happened. The joining of two quarks proved not to produce a benefit, and that project was dropped. But in a continued drive to create, three quarks united and formed the first hydrogen ion. This ion was much more complex than three times a single quark and has significantly more potential. A different type of subatomic particle, an electron, observed what was occurring and asked to join in the process. This led to the hydrogen atom. Two such atoms decided to join together, and the hydrogen molecule was created. Thus, the creative process was established, and greater complexity and functionality through joining together and corporation had started. This basic process was repeated with various types of subatomic particles, and eventually a carbon atom united with four hydrogen atoms to produce methane, the basis of organic life on earth.

Through different but similar processes, various new things were created as directed by their individual and collective primordial wisdoms. All things have this drive to create. This drive is from Absolute Source (AS). AS is both the drive to create and creation itself.

Two methane molecules found the right conditions and motivation to form ethane, which in turn led to more and more complex and specialized organic molecules. Ethane leads to ethanol, which leads to acetic acid, which eventually leads to long chain fatty acids (LCFA). Through their own intelligence and choice as well as some trial and error, different LCFA form a rudimentary membrane. Through interaction and cooperation, carbon, hydrogen, oxygen, and nitrogen atoms joined together to form amino acids, which link together to form peptides and proteins. Among many other actions, various proteins imbedded in a lipid bilayer, forming the beginning of a cell membrane.

By using the growing wisdom of various collectives and the drive to evolve into more complex and useful forms, unique molecules were generated, eventually allowing the creation of early RNA/DNA materials and the creation of carbon-based life.

Through the use of the developing greater and greater wisdom, the drive to create, and the willingness to try various experiments, disregarding what did not work or was uninteresting while retaining and building upon what seems to be a good step forward, we arrive with the plethora of interesting life forms we now experience. Something gave the smallest thing a grain of primordial wisdom, which has been utilized very wisely.

11

We Are All One

Question: What does the statement "we are all one" really mean?

In the early 1990s, a friend mentioned a massage therapist that had helped her with a chronic pain issue, and since I had had back problems for years, I decided to get an appointment with this therapist. Not only was she a superb therapist, but since we shared common spiritual interest, we became close personal friends as we discussed various ideas, books, and people. I saw her about once a month for a therapeutic massage and an interesting discussion. Shortly after the turn of the century, I started studying Shambhala Buddhism and at about the same time she started studying *A Course in Miracles.* Our intellectual interactions soon evolved into discussions and comparisons of the two areas. This continued until I moved to another state in 2011. I now reside in the Bible Belt, where there are few people willing to discuss ACIM, Buddhism, secular spirituality, etc. Because I crave being exposed to new and different spiritual views, I decided to reread ACIM. I had read the entire work (three books) in the early 1990s but did not care for it since it was written in a Christian vernacular. By 2012, I had grown to where I could easily accept the teachings of Jesus (as I understand his words, not as others tell me what I should believe they mean) and I found I now resonated with these books. ACIM actually helped me better understand and appreciate the Buddhist teachings.

One of the first things that struck me as I reread and contemplated ACIM was the teaching, "We are all one." I had heard this idea many times before and agreed with it intellectually but had little grasp of its deeper meaning and importance.

I often am reading two or three books at the same time, shifting daily from one to another. Within a week of reading the "we are all one" teaching in ACIM, I read the same concept in two secular books. When I hear the something from unrelated sources three times within a week (which frequently happens), I pay attention. I started contemplating this teaching and journeying to gain a deeper understand of what the words really meant. I have done this several times over the last five years, each time gaining a deeper appreciation of those words.

Question: How are we all one?

Guide's response: You will recall you once heard a famous atheist scientist say we are all made of stardust. You felt you understood this and agreed with the general idea. However, with study and contemplation, your consciousness evolved, and you developed a deeper appreciation. Physically all living things are made of the same materials—materials that were produced in the blast furnaces of early exploding stars. For those of you who believe there is only the physical realm, that is the entirety of it. As you (Stan) realize the existence of spirit realms, you understand there is a much more profound meaning.

While your physical bodies are made of "stardust," if you like that term, all of you (body, mind, and spirit) was created by and from Absolute Source (Creator, God) either directly or indirectly. And since there is but one Source, everyone and everything was created by Source from the same stuff. That stuff is Source itself. While you are all physically individuals, spiritually you are all creations of AS, and you should at the very minimum consider yourselves all brothers and sisters. You are all from the one, AS. You are all part of Source. As you more fully understand you all are equal and one, you will appreciate and love each other as self regardless of eye color, skin color, being left handed or right handed, being liberal or conservative, where you were born, where you live, how you worship or do not worship, your views, your attitude toward sex, etc. You are all brothers/sisters of the same family and need to love, share, help, and support each other equally.

Although I have less than a complete understanding of the teaching, "We are all one," I now feel I have a much deeper appreciation of its truth. Almost as a footnote to the above communication, I was shown a series of mental pictures depicting the biblical story about Cain slaying his brother Abel. That is not the outcome we would choose if we realized we are all one. Cain's behavior was more animal than human. This post-communication strengthens my view that unless we develop compassion, kindness, understanding, and acceptance toward all people and indeed toward all sentient beings, the earth may become a very unpleasant for *all* of us.

12

WHERE DO WE GO FROM HERE?

Question: Physical evolution has led to the era of homo sapiens, currently the most advanced physical form on earth. My question is, where do we go from here?

Guide's response: A major stimulus for physical evolution is a change in the surrounding environment. Colder or warmer temperatures, less water, less food, bigger predators, etc., require adaptation. What adapts best survives best. It is entirely possible that humans, due to overpopulation and limited resources, will revert to a primitive behavior and will destroy each other to get enough food, water, and/or energy. If you continue to view yourselves as superior and everyone else as less, you will continue to generate more hatred, discord, and violence. Hopefully increased awareness, increased wisdom, and your expanding consciousness will prevent this. Or due to your own greed, selfishness, and ignorance, you will destroy the environment and induce the annihilation of most of yourselves through your own actions. If this does occur, it might create environmental changes that will require the survivors of this self-extinction to be more intelligent and cooperative. This certainly would be a more advanced species than humans are today. Our desire is that humans will start using their brains and their hearts to consciously direct your future evolution from animal brain to human brain and beyond. If this does not occur, Gaia may need purify itself by getting rid of the human species.

Stan's thoughts: With the direction the peoples of this world seem to be taking, I have doubts that humanity will survive without major catastrophes to cause us humans to wake up and realize what we are doing to each other and to the earth. However, even if we do wake up, we will have to repair the damage we have done and to create a modernized worldwide lifestyle that permits all of us to survive on what the earth still has to offer and that allows the planet to continually renew itself (i.e., stainable existence).

Follow-Up Question 1: *What can we/I do?*

The following is my summary of a personal plan I was led to with the help of my guides and my own intellect. It represents how I am trying to evolve/expand my consciousness and to help others do likewise. You might be led to do something similar or some things that are more suited for your current mind-set, talents, and resources, which for many are far greater than mine. The important thing is to do something using your knowledge, wisdom, and intuition that you feel will have a positive impact. As we grow, we will see things differently and may be led to alter what we are doing to rectify our cosmic situation.

My guides have shown me that at my current level of understanding, the best way for me to evolve and help the earth and its sentient beings is through my thought energies. I was shown that thoughts can originate in both the brain (intellectually formed) and the mind (intuitively formed). If we energize those thoughts through intent and desire, they may become *thought forms,* which can lead to some type of physical manifestation as they go out into the universe. Therefore, it is important for me to be sure my thoughts are based on love, caring, kindness, acceptance, and understanding and not arising from selfishness, fear, anger, or negativity.

This is a challenge for me. For some reason, I became a pessimistic, angry person. As I remember, I once was a very empathetic, caring, and kind child. I was happy and thought good things would come to me as well as everyone else. It was probably when I developed diabetes (1959, age fourteen) that I changed. While many good things came my way, I started to see the ugliness of life rather than its beauty. I was starting to feel that if something could go wrong, it probably would. My motto was "hope for the best but expect the worst." Constant fear of impending doom is often a characteristic of people with ADHD, which I have, and this may be why I started to fear the future. Regardless, I tend to have more negative thoughts than positive happy ones. My positive thoughts have created or drawn into my life several wonderful things, such as new jobs, new relationships, professional successes, and athletic victories. I firmly believe that positive thinking through visualization works, but I wonder if my angry thoughts may have made my life more hellish than it otherwise might have been. Therefore, I now pay close attention to what I am thinking and try to change any negative thoughts I might have into positive ones as soon as I become aware of them.

When I see or hear of people and/or animals suffering, I send them love and light and ask that their suffering be removed and that they are comforted. Of course, I try to help physically as well as energetically. For me thoughts generated with strong intent and with visual images attached are much more than simple ideas. They have their own power and energy. I do ascribe to the saying that ideas without actions are usually not of great value, so I try to physically act to help reduce suffering as much as possible. I try to keep my ego out of my efforts as much as I can, preferring to remain anonymous and to work behind the scenes.

I also donate 10 percent of my income to five organizations that I feel are doing the best work to reduce suffering, hunger, and poor health around the world. Since I personally believe the world has many times the population it can support, I also contribute to organizations that are working to compassionately slow, stop, and reverse population growth.

Currently this is the action plan my guides and I have developed. I share it not to encourage others to do the same but to encourage them to develop their own plan to help save the human species and the world.

13

Personal Anger

Question: Why do I (Stan) have so much anger, and how can I better control it?

Currently, one of my most challenging issues is my anger. I often feel that my anger is slowing and perhaps even reversing my spiritual growth/evolution. A question I often ask my guides is how I decrease and remove anger from my internal environment. I should start by repeating that I believe there is only one absolute *truth*. I also believe that *truth* is very, very far beyond the ability of human intellect and consciousness to comprehend. Because of the distance we are from understanding what absolute *truth* might be, we will have many different views of what is true with regard to ideas, views, and beliefs. For the continued evolution of human consciousness, I believe it is important that we share our views with others and respectfully listen to their ideas. We might hear something that stimulates a new thought for us to consider, which in turn could lead to an expansion of our views. That is one way we can peacefully and painlessly evolve. While respecting the views of others and with a questioning open mind, it is important that we determine our individual views and beliefs and not accept what others say unless it resonates within our own being. What follows is how I am currently trying to work with my anger. Again, it was developed with input from my spirit guides. It is my method. It may or may not be helpful for you.

On reflection, I seem to have been a very angry person for a long time. In the environment I was raised in, anger was a principal way people interacted.

Anger often induces fear, so it can be an effective way of controlling others and getting our own way—at least until the "other" starts expressing their anger, which can lead to unpleasant results. While I currently rarely express my anger outwardly, I often think angry thoughts about getting even and/ or gaining control. These thoughts usually expressed some type of physical superiority and occasionally led to serious conflict. As I matured and found myself in situations where open physical conflict was unacceptable, my confrontations became mostly verbal, giving the image of intellectual superiority. Now, in old age, my anger is usually directed at myself for not being as physically or mentally competent as I once was. I used to be a good athlete and was not dumb. While I have often used my anger to accomplish objectives or to get others to go in the direction I thought best, I paid an emotional, physical, and spiritual price for that anger. I had always thought of myself as a caring, kind, helpful person, which I usually was. It came as a big surprise and a harsh wakeup call when I found some people, many of whom were very close to me, saw me as an intimidating, scary person. This is when I realized my internal anger was leaking out at some level. I also realized I was extremely unhappy with myself and almost everything going on around me. It then occurred to me that my anger was probably holding back my spiritual development. I realized that letting go of anger might be an important lesson I needed to learn.

For the last several years, I have tried to at least control my internal anger. I wish I could say I have been completely successful, but while I have made significant progress, I am far from being anger free. I am somewhat ashamed of my anger, so I have not talked much about it to family or friends. (Probably at some point I will have to address my *shame* issue but that will have to wait.) I have, however, talked to various psychologists and spiritual advisors about this issue. This has been helpful, but what has brought me the most success is what has been given to me in meditation and shamanic journeying. I have been advised to pay close attention to my thoughts. When angry thoughts arise, I try to not get caught up in a mental storyline where I enlarge the anger, but rather I try to recognize it and ask where it is really coming from and why I am manufacturing these thoughts. I was shown to ask myself what value this anger has—to not fan the flames of anger but rather, to just let it go. This was not to suggest suppressing the anger but to calmly allow it to dissolve. I continue to ask for help from the spirit realms, to meditate, to contemplate, and to learn about what others do to reduce anger. My anger is much less than it once was. I hope that I will have mastered it by the time I end my current physical journey.

Question: How do I better deal with my anger?

Guides' response: My guides suggested that I first stop "being angry about being angry." When I lose my temper, either outwardly or internally, I feel angry at myself and thereby double my anger quotient. If I stop this anger at anger, I reduce my hostility and can focus on redirecting the energy of my initial anger in a more positive direction.

14

Becoming a Better Person

Question: How can I be a better person (i.e., how can I produce more positive karma)?

When I reflect on my life's path, I often feel I have acted inappropriately and at times caused pain. I never did this knowingly, but often I think I have brought more misery into the world than happiness. I had what the Buddhists call a good rebirth into this life. Westerners would call it a privileged birth. Maybe the situation I was born into was due to positive merit generated in past lives, or maybe it was just chance. In the past, I questioned if I had wasted my talents and opportunities. I asked myself if I had done all I could to be happy and to help others be happy. Was I a giving person, or was I selfish and self-centered? Over the past five years, my number one priority has been to identify how I can be of benefit to others, to society, and to the world. I have asked psychics to contact my spirit guides/friends to see what they (the psychics) could hear, see, or feel about my efforts to be a better person. Most often they heard that I should be patient and just keep trying. That did not satisfy me. Then I was given the thought that I was my own best contactor of my spirit helpers and I should ask them myself. So I did.

Question: Where should I serve and what should I do to become a better person and to make the world a better place?

I asked this question several times, and here is a brief summary of the responses.

First, I saw an image of what I guess was one of my spirit advisors who was laughing. It said, "Lighten up, Stan. Stop with all the worry. You are what you are. You're doing what you're doing. It could be no other way." Than its laughter turned into a smirk. It knew I wanted and expected more than that. The next week I asked for clarification.

Follow-up Request 1: Thank you for your response, but I really want to know specifically what would be best for me to do now.

My smirking spirit friend then showed/told me that *it* knew I was sincere in my desire to do the right thing and that I was not at all sure I knew what the right thing was. I was shown that I usually tried to identify the most appropriate action and I then acted accordingly, except for those times when my anger overwhelmed me. I did the best I could to be of benefit. I was further shown that all my opportunities and all the choices I made are what brought me to this place at this time. I could be nowhere else. I was told that this was where I was supposed to be. Maybe future opportunity and choice would move me someplace else, maybe not. I was reminded the future is not fixed, there is always free will, and I am perfect for who/what I am, and I am still learning. I will continue to make good decisions and less-than-good decisions, but I will always try to do my best. I will continue to learn from what I label as successes and from what I label as failures. And I often will not be able to tell my failures from my successes. I was then shown that success and failure were just opposite sides of the same coin, and one could not exist without the other. I was asked to realize there are missed opportunities but there are not mistakes. You can learn from missed opportunities as well as from successes and failures.

About three months later, I was journeying on a different subject when my guide(s) appeared in my mind and said: "We have been suggesting for over three of your years that it would be good for you to share some of the nonpersonal information we have given you. This will complete a significant segment of your lifetime path. Your ego is trying to sabotage you causing you to feel you cannot do this. It wants you to stay in body as long as possible because when you leave your body, it will no longer exist. We think that sharing our communications with others might be one of your last major contributions.

"Rather than just leaving all the 'journey journals' you have recorded from our visits for your loved ones to decipher after you transition, you should put them in a typed book form. No one can read your handwriting, and you misspell a lot of words. You have spell-check on your computer which, will help you." I am now following my friends' advice.

Follow up question 2: *Okay, I am where I am and doing what I am doing, but still I would like to get as far along my spiritual path as I can so I will transition into the highest level or vibrational frequency as I possibly can. What can I do to cause this?*

The laughing image form again appeared and said, "It would be good for you to relax and give up worry. It's a lesson you can now learn if you choose. You will go to the level that best fits your experiences and what you have learned from those experiences. It would make no sense for you to go to a lower vibration level. You already know what you can learn at that frequency. If you were to go to a higher frequency than appropriate, you would be uncomfortable, and it would be difficult for you to understand the teachings that are given there."

I was then shown my early days at Vanderbilt University when I thought all the other staff members knew a lot more than I did and feared being fired if the department chairman found out how dumb I actually was. It was not a very comfortable place for me until my research success helped me realize I was a more than adequate scientist. I was reassured by my now-smiling guide that I had worked hard in this life and have grown as opportunities opened for me. I would go to the level that is the most pleasant for me, where I can receive the highest teachings I am able to comprehend. So I guess I will accept my friend's advice, close this section, and see what happens next. Love and blessings.

15

What Has the Highest Priority?

Question: Given my current situation, what is the most important/beneficial thing I can do to help both myself and others to evolve spiritually?

Communication from my guides: I was shown that I needed to have faith and confidence in myself and in my internal wisdom. When I still myself for a moment, I will know the best thing to say and/or do when a situation or opportunity presents itself. It was stressed that my contribution would have a greater positive impact if I remembered we are all one, from the one Source, and to remove any selfish thoughts my ego might generate. It was stressed I should always use kindness, compassion, intellect, and most importantly, intuition and not animalistic instinct to direct my actions.

Follow-up Question 1: *Often a situation will occur, and my first response is anger. At times, I may want to argue or fight. I might even want to destroy what I see as wrong or blocking the path I think we should travel. How can I change this response?*

Communication from guides: I was told that when I start to feel anger, it is instinct, and I would benefit from slowing down and becoming calm—the old advice to count to ten, I guess. I should stop and listen to my internal guidance. This will allow the most appropriate response to be revealed to me.

I was also shown that I have many strong preferences and desires and that I usually feel I see the best way to go about things. But these preferences are mine alone and might not be what is best for others. If is fine to pursue my wishes as long as I do it peacefully without trying to push my views on others. People have to find their own path. If they make a poor decision, they will suffer from that decision and will learn to correct it. That is one way growth occurs. Sharing views and positions is good, but if I try to push my views on others, it can produce more anger from them and from me.

I was counseled to not become a prisoner to my views and beliefs and to not respond out of habit. I was advised to think and to consider all options before I say or do anything. Before I respond, I need to be sure I am coming from a center of love, peace, understanding, and acceptance. My beliefs, views, habits, and preferences will change as my spirit evolves. I should be careful to allow this to happen organically. This will allow me to embrace new and better views that will help me become wiser and more compassionate.

16

FEAR

Question: Why has my life been so negatively impacted by fear?

Communication from my guides: At the current level of human evolution, fear is a major limiting emotion. In your personal life (Stanley's), it has been more limiting than anger since the energy of anger can be used for accomplishment. Fear can only be used to limit, control, and destroy. Parents often think they can use fear to help protect their children. In actual fact, they are more often than not suppressing the growth, development, and creativity of their children by using fear to influence and control. Religions uses the fear of eternal damnation to control their believers. Power-hungry politicians use fear to divide and control voters and thereby, win elections. Fear reduces risk-taking and slows advancement in all areas. Fear is a powerful weapon that is used to manipulate others and self. Yes, you use fear on yourselves to create conflict and generate an enemy that you use to justify your inhumane actions.

At times caution can be appropriate. Caution is based on observation, analysis, and evaluation. It can help avoid situations that may put you in jeopardy. This is particularly true when you follow your intuition. Fear is used as a negative to create division and to control. Try not to associate with or be influenced by people or organizations that induce a feeling of fear. They are probably trying to gain control over you.

My thoughts after reflection on what was shown: I personally have always been a fearful person. Fear more or less controlled my life until the pain of living in constant fright became unbearable and I decided to ignore it or at least create the image that I was not affected by it. To some extent, I just did not care what the consequences were. I also was practicing the directive, "Fake it till you make it." Perhaps that was not the most authentic way to go about life, but it often worked for me.

17

DESIRE, CRAVING, GRASPING

At various times in my life, I have heard the words *desire*, *craving*, and *grasping* called bad, evil, sinful, immoral, animalistic, and the cause of all suffering. A few years ago, I read someone who suggested that our desires were an expression of God's will. I do not believe any of these views are correct, but I do understand why some people describe them as such.

In the little church that I grew up in, desire was often associated with sexual desire. It appeared much of the somewhat hypocritical congregation viewed sex as dirty and distasteful but necessary for procreation. It was acceptable only under the marriage contract. Premarital sex was a significant sin. Having the desire was considered almost as inappropriate as the act itself.

While sexual desire was a major concern in my community, most if not all physical desires were considered wrong. To desire more than what one had was seen as inappropriate. Most of the general public seemed to believe that God gave everyone what they deserved and to want more was going against God's wishes. The desire to possess body adornments such as fancy or brightly colored clothes or jewelry was considered prideful and therefore wrong.

When I started questioning everything I heard or read, I determined that ideas like these made no logical sense, disregarded them, and lived my life accordingly. I did attempt to keep my views and actions as private as I could, only rarely sharing them. When I first heard the view that our desires are actually the projection of God's will through us, I was initially surprised, thinking God or as I would say Absolute Source probably had no interest or concern about my sex life or what clothes I chose to wear. I felt the view that desire was a projection of God's will to be as incorrect as it being a sin. The wise author who expressed the God's will view eventually went on to say any desire that comes from an altruistic core (selflessness, compassion, kindness, wisdom, etc.) is God's will working through us. The more animalistic desires (dominance, hatred, manipulation, violence, etc.) are leftovers from our lives as four-legged beings. Upon reflection, I embraced this concept. Eventually I began to realize that Absolute Source, which is *all*, probably does not need or have an attribute such as "will" and rejected desire as being God's will but could see it might be my higher self's will. Still being confused about desire, I thought it wise to get a higher-level opinion.

Question: Are having desires helpful or a hindrance? Is desire good or bad, right or wrong, to be embraced or avoided?

Guide's response: You would best benefit by first seeing it (desire but extending to include craving and grasping) as a word with no morality attached to it. That view can be extended to include "the state of" but not the action generated from that state. Actions are the effects arising from the "state of" and do produce moral consequences. Desire is a major force for creation. We are not referring to mating desire and the production of offspring, which is usually more of an instinctual drive. We say usual because sex is most often the result of a lusting energy that can generate pleasure and is appropriate as long as there is no force, coercion, or deceit involved. But sexual union can also generate a form of completion in the physical realm. In many things, there exist masculine and feminine energies that are different and complementary. They form two distinct polarities. Coming together and merging the feminine and masculine brings about a perfect balance of the initial polarization and a state of completion. Focusing on all desire and not only the mating or completing aspects will lead you to realize the importance of desire in the creation of all things both beneficial and destructive. You can have a desire for a new home, which, after planning, saving money, and securing building materials, you can create. Having the new home could have positive, negative, or neutral consequences. You could also have a desire to help the needy and start supporting a local food bank to ease the hunger problem. You probably would view that as a positive consequence. You could have the desire that someone you dislike or who you consider an enemy experiences misfortune or death. This most often would be a negative result of your desire. You (Stan) personally would benefit if you stop trying to characterize everything and to focus on intent.

Craving and grasping can be viewed in a similar fashion. Craving could be looked at as a more severe form of desire—a physiological need rather than an emotion one. If you went without water for a day, you would crave water. If you could not experience that craving and did not drink fluid, you would soon die. Here craving is beneficial. Craving power over others, more resources for yourself regardless of the consequences, and drugs or alcohol would be examples of craving being negative.

It is hoped you can now easily see how there are times to grasp or hold onto something and times to release it.

Depending on the situation and your intent, desiring, craving, and grasping can be appropriate, inappropriate, or neutral.

18

JUST THE NEXT STEP

One morning after my normal reading period, I did my meditation practice and then journeyed to the spirit realm, asking for general guidance and specifically how I could advance along my life's spiritual path faster and/or further. I met my ascended master, guide, and friend Jesus. He had the same appearance as the picture that hung in the front of the country church I attended for the first eighteen years of my life, staff and all.

He put His arm around my shoulder and said, "You would like to see the end of your journey—to see all you have created and the impact of your journey on others, both positive and negative. But by setting a final definite endpoint to any endeavor, particularly your life's path, you limit yourself and your contributions. If you have or see a definite endpoint, that will be the best you can do. If you allow an undefined stopping point (i.e., death), you will accomplish more because you will make better decisions concerning your next step as you mature spiritually and evolve.

"You (Stan) like to visualize using the two hemispheres of your brain (see part 3 for various mental activities and thought processes). So, to have a clearer awareness, go with your right hemisphere style of realization, and using your intuition, natural wisdom, constructive imagery, and desire, listen for direct guidance when you meditate and journey. Ask what your next step should be. You will be guided. You can then use your left-brain hemisphere with its talents of reason, logic, analysis, and knowledge to develop a clear plan related to your next step. We will guide you in the most appropriate direction.

19

LIFE IN THE SPIRIT REALM

Question: What will my existence be like after transitioning to the spirit realm?

Response: One morning after my usual spiritual practices, I journeyed to the spirit realm to ask my ascendant master (the energy that appears as Jesus) what I could expect after my next physical death. I was shown that after the normal transition process, which would be an extension of my NDE, I would be greeted by friends who had transitioned earlier, my guides, and various other helping spirits. After an adjustment period and life review,[1] I would move to a place where I could continue my learning and evolution. I was told that I could best understand the characteristics of this place by visualizing it as having a certain vibrational frequency appropriate for my level of consciousness. This would be a level where I would be most comfortable and where I could best continue my development. Other spirits with similar levels of maturation would also reside there. My

---

[1] A life review was shown to be different from what many people have experienced during a NDE or through channeling. It was much less about the good and bad behaviors I exhibited while in the physical realm and primarily dependent on the degree to which I had mastered the lessons I had reincarnated to experience and learn. Also, part of the review was the extent to which I had interacted with other incarnated spirits as we had agreed on prior to physical birth. With free will we sometimes decide to not complete all the lessons we originally agreed to and may not have played as great a role in other spirits' earthly journey as was expected. I was also shown incarnate spirits can take on extra learning in the physical realm if they so choose.

particular vibrational level would depend on the lessons I had learned and my interest.[2] I was shown that since I enjoy and easily learned through study, exploration, reflection, and discussion, that I would be in close communion with other spirits with similar preferences and understanding.

---

[2] This is similar to what is communicated in the next question. (See chapter 20.)

20

DIFFERENT LEVELS

Question: Are there different levels in the spirit realm, and if so, what can I do while in the physical realm to enable me to transition to a higher vibration level when I die?

Response (First I was jokingly chastised as my guides communicated.): You (Stan) should lighten up. Maybe you might benefit by not being so driven to attempt to identify what you can do now (physical realm) to allow you to gain a higher level when you transition. You are projecting a human earthly characteristic, the drive to get ahead or as you like to say, "move up the ladder," into the spirit realm. Your intentions are good, but it does not exactly work that way. Just do the best you can at all things. Try to be aware and listen to your intuition. The energy of creation, you might wish to say karma, will deliver you to where you need to go to maximize your continued growth in the Spirit Realm. As we have often told you, there is no punishment, unless you choose to punish yourself, and there is nothing to fear. *(I was also shown that massively evil people go to a very, very low vibrational level where there is little or no joy. It takes them a great deal of work [reflection, understanding, and forgiveness of themselves] to even start to move into higher levels).*

There are many realms and many levels in each realm. Most earthly humans see things as black or white, good or bad, right or wrong. They believe the more good they do versus the bad they create, the better place they will go to when they die. Some humans believe there are only two nonphysical realms, heaven and hell. These people are usually strong believers in punishment and reward. Again, that is not how it works. The more evolved your consciousness is, the more you will desire to create things of benefit for both yourself and others. You will desire to not create (do) things that bring harm to others, even if you personally might derive some short-term benefit. Humans whose consciousness is not very evolved will be selfish and will do things that they feel will help them regardless of the impact on others. When you let go of your physical body, you will transition into the realm and level that is most suited for you based on your understanding, desires, abilities, qualities, and energies. The last term, *energies*, may or may not have meaning to you, but do not be concerned. You will go where you will be most at home and happy.

It is noble and good to put the right effort into everything you undertake. A problem for you (Stan) is that you do not always realize what is the right effort and what is not enough or too much. You need to be a bit more balanced and patient. Trying to go to fast may cause errors and take you off your path. Of course, going too slow is not good either. You are late in this life, and you do not believe you ever want to be in the physical realm again. Because of this, you want to get it all done now. We tell you, you always have a choice whether to take on form or to remain in spirit, and while there is no such thing as time, you never get it all done. But thanks for trying.[3]

---

[3] A little humor from my spirit friends to begin and end this communication.

21

SELF-HEALING

Question: Why have I not been able to heal myself?

I had difficulty deciding whether to include the following material in part 2 or part 3 or not include it at all. It is of a very personal and individual nature, so I originally thought it would fit best in part 3. However, I did my normal ritual to get information from my guides (meditation, contemplation, journeying, semiautomatic writing) and the information conveyed appears to have deeper meaning, so I was led to include it in part 2. As usual the information was shown to me in a fashion I could understand at my current level of consciousness. I need to point out that I believe we all have a general life plan. I also have a superficial understanding of quantum theory. Both of these definitely influenced the way the guides answered my question.

Question: For the last several years, I have had a spiritual practice of sending energy, which I refer to as LoveLight, to people or areas in need. For the last sixteen months, I have been sending energy to my foot in an effort to speed its healing. This has not appeared to help, and I have now had a total of three toes removed. *Does this mean that my LoveLight practice is worthless—that I am an ineffective light worker or what?* (Currently, my foot appears to be healing, so maybe I am just slow rather than ineffective.)

Guide's response: There are several different views we can point out to respond to this question. First, we want to communicate that for the last five years, the way you have been of service to others, including Gaia, has been to do what you call LoveLight practice. Since you experienced the golden-white cloud of love during your NDE, you have a wonderful awareness to visualize and bring LoveLight into yourself and then project it to those in need. We encourage you to continue your practice. It helps you to be of service. Remember, you have always been able to use your gifts in service to others more than for yourself.

Currently your primary focus is to type out (*due to my unreadable handwriting—my comment*) some of the information we have communicated to you. You probably would never have taken time away from the physical activities you so enjoyed had you not been incapacitated. So the manuscript you now are so involved with owes its existence to your health issues. We are happy you are sharing some of our communications but hope you realize that we are not involved in your state of health. It would be very incorrect to see your issues as a punishment or a manipulation to persuade you to write the manuscript. We suggest you should view your activities as an expression of your free will. We cannot say, but at some level of awareness you may have made the decision to now step away (Stan's thought: *sounds like a bad pun from my guide guys*) from what you had been doing and to write. We know you have had the desire to write for some time but thought you were incapable. Now that you have little other involvement with your old world, you feel you might as well take a shot. These are all your decisions and not those of higher energies.

We also point out that you have a life plan and have complete free will. Perhaps all of this is just part of that plan. Since you always ask for things you do to serve the highest purpose, this quite possibly is what you agreed to before reincarnation as Stan.

You have a vision of what quantum theorists refer to as a probability wave used to describe the momentum of very small subatomic particles, such as an electron.[4] You might like to view your life as a set of probability waves. Nothing is really certain. There is just a probability that something will or will not occur. Your thoughts, desires, and beliefs can collapse a probability wave into a certainty. We realize you have a level of fear that your foot will not heal and you will require an additional amputation. You can view fear as something that can collapse your life's waves into an unpleasant certainty. We advise you to let go of all fear as best you can.

We would be pleased if you continue your LoveLight work and your writing, but those decisions are completely yours.

---

[4] My limited understanding of quantum mechanics is that ultra-small particles are more like waves representing probabilities that they will behave in a certain way. When that particle is observed or measured, that wave collapses into a specific location.

22

ENERGY

The topic of energy was not an area I had originally considered including in this book, but my guides seemed very insistent that I do so. They kept raising the question below over and over again in my mind until I finally agreed to put it through my meditation, contemplation, journey ritual. I do not understand their information as well as I usually do but hopefully others will.

Question: Is it true that energy can neither be created nor destroyed?

Guide's response: As always, we first have to determine what you mean by energy, created, and destroyed. The physical realm is a special and relatively limited state. Physical laws like energy can be neither created nor destroyed, the speed of light in a vacuum, etc., usually are true within the limits of people's ability to measure and/or understand. They provide a solid framework in which various theories can be tested and proved or disproved. But energy in the spirit realm (spiritual energy) can come into being (created) or cease to be (destroyed) at will. In the physical realm energy is defined as the ability to do work (move, build, destroy) or generate heat. You (Stan) believe that thoughts, when energized by intent, can cause or at least help make things occur or not occur. (Have you ever considered the power or energy of a wave of love?) There is some validity to the paradigm that you can attract things to you like relationships, friendships, and opportunities or to develop a deeper intuitive awareness.

This type of creating or growing does not take physical energy but utilizes spiritual energy.

At your (*Stan's*) level of consciousness, it would be beneficial to see what you call mind (*distinct from brain*) as a bridge connecting the spiritual realm and the physical realm. This bridge can allow spiritual energy to flow into and affect the physical world. This is how the power of thought sometimes works, with spiritual energy flowing through the mind and affecting the physical. You sometimes refer to the result as a miracle. At many of the initial spirit levels, it is viewed as there being an infinite source that can call energy into being (create) or to disappear (destroyed) when no longer needed. A better way to describe spiritual energy would be to think of it "being" when needed and "not being" when no longer needed. With this spiritual energy, spirit can create any environment or form its wishes for as long as it so desires. A spirit that has recently moved into the nonphysical realm will create earthly scenes, but this desire quickly fades. Ultimately all energy comes from Absolute Source and can be directed by the free will of spirit beings.

Physical existence could be compared to becoming an artist working with the special and unique medium of matter. You learn to create by manipulating matter using physical energy. We are not limiting this to just artistic pursuits but to all things. As you develop the abilities to create, your creations will have increasing impact on your world.

Because of your (Stan) very pleasant NDE, you believe the physical realm is inferior to the spirit realms. A more correct view would be to describe the physical realm as limited. There you can have experiences and learn lessons that you could not completely appreciate in any of the spirit realms. That is why you created your physical experience. When you have completed your journey, you will take all learning and the appreciation of that learning to the spirit realm, which will cause that realm to grow and evolve.

23

SELFISHNESS

Question: It seems to me that in this world there are a lot of people who want more than their fair share regardless of the consequences. Why are some people so uncompassionate and selfish?

Guide's communication: We understand you get really pissed off[5] when you observe unkind, destructive behavior. At your current level of consciousness, you see where this type of behavior will lead if not corrected. The people exhibiting these behaviors are ignorant of the consequences of their beliefs and actions. We say "beliefs" because they often believe their actions are appropriate. View it as a bell-shaped curve where the greatest percentage

---

[5] Dear Sir Stan of Le, as you previously liked to call yourself (good that you have at least some sense of fun). Here is a little extra just for you. We intentionally used that term because you sometimes feel guilty when you use "naughty" words (we are trying to make you laugh). You should stop with all this guilt stuff! Harsh words when used to the appropriate degree are often a clearer way of communicating. Your guilt about the use of certain words is your ignorance. These are what you call old tapes from early imprinting. They were words older people did not like you to say, so they called their usage a sin. You still carry a lot of useless baggage from your early indoctrination. You were taught social politeness by your parents, and you really dislike offending others (more early imprinting). While being considerate of other people's feelings, it would be best that you not feel you have done something wrong when you choose to live by your rules and not the desires of others. Usually, as in not always, it's appropriate to be inoffensive. When are you going to drop all this guilt stuff?

of the population is near the middle of the curve. Some individuals are leading the curve and have a better understanding of the situation the human race has now put itself in. There is also an equal number of people lagging the curve because they still hold onto old, antiquated views and belief. Currently you have a clearer vision of where the mind-set of the majority is taking humanity than many.

We counsel you that you are responsible for your behavior and not the behaviors of others. You will be impacted by the directions the world's people move in, and you need do what you can to help others wake up. Because of your life path agreement, you are obligated to help and to advise others if they are ready to listen and want your help. If humanity does not destroy itself, eventually the consciousness of the majority will evolve to the level where the current non-caring attitude will no longer be acceptable to the majority. As most of the great spiritual reformers of your era have requested, be the best person you can and always seek greater understanding. Other people will change at their own pace.

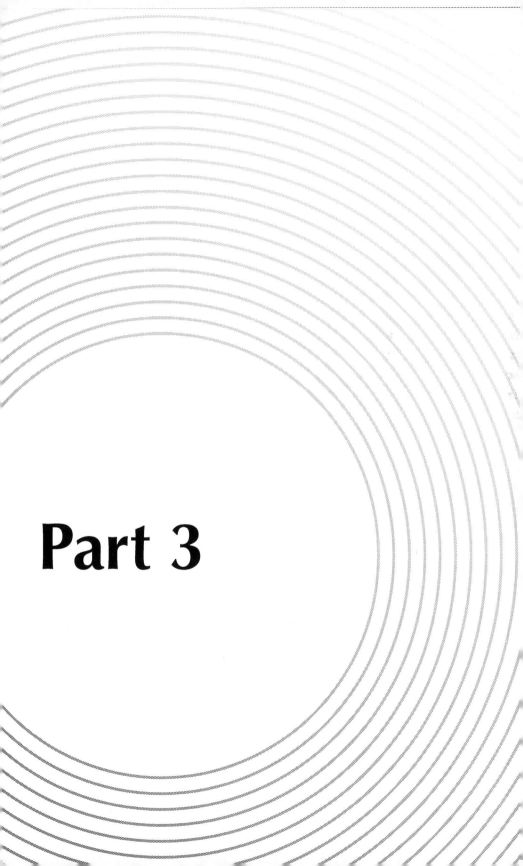

Part 3

Views, Thoughts, Ideas

Part 3 is similar to part 2 except I do not know how much of the material came from the spirit realm and how much came from me. Rather than asking my spirit guides and teachers specific questions and then journeying to receive the answers, the material in part 3 came to me without specifically requesting it. I was always (or almost always) in a very relaxed state when I received the material, neither trying to think or trying not to think. Often I would be relaxing with a glass of wine on my large deck, looking out at the woods, and often observing various small animals and the occasional deer when a thought would appear. Usually I would pay little or no attention. Occasionally I would allow the thought to linger in my mind and start adding additional thoughts to it. The initial or triggering thought often came in the form of a question that then proceeded to answer or explain itself. My thoughts were always of a philosophical nature and not mere fantasy. I would allow the thought to play in my mind, and it would take on a picture like quality. I am not sure where the material came from, but often it made sense to me and I would incorporate that new understanding into my philosophy and life. I will list a short verbal description of the various visuals I was given or created (or perhaps both). Again, the construction, whether it is from my guides or from my own mind, is in the form that I can best understand and utilize.

24

WHERE, WHEN, AND HOW DID MY SPIRIT COME INTO BEING?

Question/thought: I have a spirit, but what exactly is my spirit and where did it manifest from? Was it always as it is now, or has it evolved? Are spirit and soul the same thing?

In my mind, these three questions are related, and I thought and explored them as a single unit.

Because of the way my brain functions (brain and mind are *not* the same thing to me, which I will discuss later), I visualize my thoughts as images, sometimes amorphous, sometimes more concrete. I usually think and visualize in terms of energy—moving, flowing, and reforming energy(s). It is difficult to articulate, but I see my mental visions as energy constructs. I do not have the ability to see auras, but I can often feel or sense the emotional energy of a person.

I believe all that is comes from Absolute Source. I usually picture Source as working through energy(s). For now, I will leave the term *energy* undefined. I am not certain I know what I really mean when I say "energy." It is just how I picture things. In the series of questions above, the first add-on image was a large molten sea of energy. As planet earth was formed, some energy manifested as matter (mineral) and some as the spirit of that matter. As used here, energy is not necessarily a thing (substance, force, etc.) but whatever Absolute Source chooses to manifest as to get the process started. I could not tell if there was one spirit for all earthly matter or if various bits and pieces of matter each had their own specific spirit. With time, some of the inorganic matter changed into or joined with organic material and eventually become plants. It appeared to me that each individual plant has its own consciousness or spirit. Plant spirit/consciousness evolved to become the spirits of fish, then reptiles, then birds, then mammals, and finally humans. I saw the evolution of spirit occurring by two processes. The first was what I would call straightforward evolution where the consciousness expands thought its own growth (i.e., it learns). The second is by the merging of two or more compatible lower-vibrational consciousnesses, leading to a single higher-level spirit. It would be inaccurate to see a single isolated individual spirit evolving from mineral through vegetable into animal and finally into human. Their initial energy(s) can be modified in numerous ways as they advance to higher and higher vibrational states.

As for spirit and soul, it would depend on your point of view and belief. I prefer the term *spirit*. Soul can give the impression that it is something that is fixed and static, whereas spirit is a dynamically growing composite of energies.

25

Life Plan

Question/thought: Life plan or no life plan?

On a late September afternoon in 2015, I sat on my deck sipping a glass of very delicious pinot grigio and pondered a recurring question of mine: Does my life have a specific plan or is there no plan? This question is related to another question I often think about: Does my life have a specific purpose? Maybe they are the same question. As you can tell from the information I shared in part 2 of this book, I have been told there is a purpose to life and that is "to evolve, to become greater, and to manifest more wisely."

My spirit guides tell me there is a general plan full of lessons we have agreed to learn and a general direction to our spiritual growth and evolution. How we accomplish that plan (or do not accomplish that plan) is up to us (i.e., free will). I am grateful for this answer and accept it, but still I keep asking myself (not my guides) about this plan, what is it really, what if I do not complete it, how will I know when I have completed it (i.e. death), or could I decide to add more to my plan? My hope is to develop an expanded view and understanding as to why a spiritual being like myself would choose to incarnate into the physical realm. Or perhaps I did not choose it. But there goes free will, so for now I choose to believe in free will and that I agreed to take on an earthly existence.

So I ask the question, is there a plan? Is there a purpose? Two possible answers immediately come to mind—no, there is not and yes, there is a life plan.

If there is no plan, it does not matter what we do or do not do, what we accomplish, what we take, or what we give. There are no eternal consequences. We would be completely free to allow our lives to unfold and accept whatever happens because soon it will end, and we will no longer exist. Many brilliant people who are driven to make great contributions to science, government, the arts, etc., have this view. I personally could not be so driven and to often make huge personal sacrifices to make a beneficial contribution if I thought there was not plan or purpose to my life. If people cling to the idea that existence ceases with physical death, what causes them to want to make the world a better place?

If I accept the view that life does have a plan, I then ask who developed that plan: my higher self, a higher governing being, Absolute Source, or what/who? For now, I believe what many incarnate spiritual writers and mystics seem to agree on, that we, with the guidance of a group of advanced spirits, formulate the plan before we incarnate. If there is a specific plan, we would want to accomplish that plan to the best of our abilities since that would be the primary purpose to incarnate. If we do not remember the plan after we reincarnate, we would need help, guidance, and protection as we transverse the physical experience. If correct, that would allow us to accept life as it develops and to rely on our intuition as well as our intellect and experience to receive guidance in learning whatever lessons are being presented to us. This would allow us to be at ease with the apparent ups and downs of life, accept events, and then respond accord to our wisdom and intuition.

Over the next several days, I asked for and received information from my guides about my views of life's plan. I include it here rather than in part 2 for the sake of clarity and flow.

Guide's communication: The best way for you (me) to understand is to accept that there is a specific plan for your life and that it was designed to give you an opportunity to master certain lessons beneficial to your spiritual growth. Your spiritual guides or angels are always with you, and you can hear them through your intuition and meditation. We understand you physical need to categorize everything and to think dualistically. Eventually you will evolve beyond those processes and realize there is no plan and that there is not no plan (i.e., you will have moved from your current dualistic reality to a nondual sphere). This will require you to develop a greater nondualistic appreciation than you currently possess. Remember, all is one. In your current way of thinking, you need opposites, plan versus no plan. But at a higher vibrational level, you will understand without the need for opposites. What you see is what you look for. We realize this is beyond your current abilities to understand, but you have a rudimentary internal awareness of this reality. This would be a topic for future meditation and contemplation.

26

Does Absolute Source (God) Think?

Question/Thought: Does Absolute Source (or God if you prefer) think? Do I think like Absolute Source does?

A friend once sarcastically said, "We have created God in our image." Even though I had moved away from my early religious training, I was momentarily taken back by his comment. After a quick reflection, I realized this was true for many people. This was 1967, and many churchgoing people sincerely felt God was really *big* but like us with two arms, two legs, ten fingers, a long white beard, and a very well-muscled male body. These people also gave their God human attitudes and thought processes. They believed God had a bigger version but similar brain. They thought he observed, analyzed, and judged as they did but in an infinitely broad fashion. Their God also had a much bigger arsenal to punish those who displeased him.

A few years later a companion said she thought of God as a spirit and we were created in spirit like him (God was still male I guess). At the time, this made some sense, but after years of spiritual searching to view God as a spirit seemed to limit God to a category that did not resonate with me and so I looked deeper.

I had a very wonderful spiritual experience during my NDE. I was embraced by the most wonderful loving light, which was beyond what I could imagine. I can easily visualize that light as being a very advanced high vibrational spiritual being, but I do not believe it was Absolute Source. To me Absolute Source is not person-like or thing-like. *It* can manifest as anything and everything but is formless and does not need to think (as "to think" is currently defined). *It* is beyond thought. It is beyond everything. *It* does not think, reason, analyze, or judge. These processes are a human construct, and it is very difficult for us humans to comprehend anything that is so superior that there is no need or use for human-like mentation. It is as to think beyond thinking. After years of studying Eastern thought on nonduality, I have a crude and probably confused feeling about how this could be. To even begin appreciating nonduality, I have to stop rational thought and embrace the undefined absolute. If you find this crazy, I completely understand. I enjoy abstract amorphous thinking. There is never a wrong (or correct) end, and it definitely is not for everyone. I completely respect how you choose to view your God. I like my view but cannot possibly articulate much if anything about it.

I feel that my guides had significant input into the above material. I did not specifically ask for information, so the material may be just the ramblings of a confused old man or maybe my guides just wanted to play a joke on me.

Stan's comments: The thoughts or nonthought described above occurred over a brief five-minute period. I had such an enjoyable time trying to conceptualize advanced energies that are beyond the need to think that I decided to take a quick look at how I think. This inquiry took a much longer period of time, which may suggest I got little help from my guides but perhaps when I focused on myself I could not hear them.

There is a lot of discussion about brain and mind. My belief is that the brain and mind are not the same thing, with the brain being something the mind can utilize if it chooses. The brain is completely contained within the physical body; the mind is not so limited. The mind may be a communication conduit between the physical and spirit realms. There is no proof of this, but I can see the possibility.

My normal way of attempting to understanding nonmaterial concepts is to try to visualize them as a physical construct. This is something my guides have cautioned me about, but at that time, I was not trying to interact with them. I was just allowing my mind (or maybe just my brain) to run wild and see where it took me. I started to think about thinking. I am not a brain scientist and have little knowledge in that area but have always been fascinated with how thoughts arise and how they might be controlled and utilized in creating or manifesting. I semi-understand that the human brain has two hemispheres that have different functions. The two sides are connected and can work together at times or somewhat independently at other times. The left hemisphere is utilized for what I think of as hard thought processes like planning, rational thinking, analyzing, and critical thought. The right hemisphere is used for intuition, holistic viewing, nonlinear thought, creativity, and imagination. In occupations like engineering, the left hemisphere is usually dominate. Artist, poets, and musicians use the right hemisphere more. That is about the end of my brain knowledge.

By chance, blessing, or curse, I seem to be able to utilize either hemisphere and can, to some extent, direct which side I would like to dominate at a particular time. This could be viewed as not being able to use either side very well. I am not detail-oriented enough to be an engineer, and I cannot paint, write poetry, sing, or play a musical instrument. I am very good at visualizing how to synthesize complex organic molecules, how the various biochemical pathways in the body work, and how different body organs function together to maintain homeostasis. I am also skilled at logic, higher forms of mathematics (but not arithmetic), and abstract reasoning. I have great difficulty understanding directions, remembering people's names, and spelling. You win some, you lose some, and some are rained out.

Those who know me know I love to discuss things from differing perspectives (debate and argument). Because of my logic, analytical, and reasoning talents coupled with relatively good listening skills (left hemisphere activities), I usually can find holes in opposing arguments, which I can then politely point out. I find this type of activity very enjoyable, but it is not the best way to make new friends. When I meet a person with similar left hemisphere skills and a love of argument, we can have an exciting and informative time. They can identify holes, errors, or inconsistencies in my views as I can in theirs. This leads to reanalysis and modification of our views. To me this represents an enjoyable way to grow.

At times when I am in a discussion on a topic I know little about, I find myself asking questions or giving an opinion without much, if any, analytical thought. There is no analysis, logical projection, or thought synthesis. My statements just self-arise. I believe when I realize I do not have sufficient knowledge or information to contribute to the discussion from my rational, linear, analytical left hemisphere, I switch to the intuitive, imaginative right hemisphere. Here my comments are usually not a continuation to what had been said but rather suggests a different view of the topic under discussion. This in turn often brings new insight to the discussion.

When I predominately utilize my logical left brain, my contribution is often sound, clear, and easily understood. I also usually feel drained and exhausted after the discussion and need time to recover and reenergize. This was the thinking mode I usually used when I worked (Director of Strategic Research), and I tried to always have a recovery hour or so between meetings that I felt might be confrontational.

Nowadays (I retired in 2002) I prefer using my right hemisphere during discussions. It seems that thinking and speaking from my right brain is very spontaneous, with no need to evaluate the impact of what I say before I speak. When I am using my right brain, my contributions are often deeper, more honest, more insightful, and usually much more impactful.

I am sure I use both hemispheres most of the time. I also believe the right hemisphere is where our intuition resides. I can easily visualize it being the physical-nonphysical connection between realms. This is just how I currently imagine it to be. It may be completely incorrect, but it gives me interesting ideas to ponder.

27

WHAT CREATED ME?

Question/thought: Did Absolute Source create the physical me?

If Absolute Source created creation so *it* could expand, evolve, and become more, it seems likely to me that *it* did not provide a lot of rules and directions. Maybe a few like the drive to evolve and/or to strive to become better but not many more. As discussed in part 2, I believe my guides showed me a scenario where humans are now the earthly leaders in our own evolution and that of the earth itself, which I view as a living being. Absolute Source started its own evolution, which eventually led to the universe, to physical life, and most recently, to us (humans). One evening while relaxing, I wondered if AS had a direct involvement in the development my physical existence or did it create the initial conditions that led to my spirit self (SS) and then perhaps it was/is my SS that is responsible for my physical manifestation. This led me to ask if AS formed me from *its* own essence (AS stuff, i.e., spirit). Perhaps it is my SS that creates and evolves in its goal to become more, which adds to AS. Maybe it's my SS that has the goal of adding to the perfect and complete AS as *it* evolves beyond perfect completeness. Perhaps my SS then manifested the physical me to learn the human qualities of compassion, caring, wisdom, and selflessness and can then use those energies in the spirit realm for further evolution of my spiritual consciousness.

I started to consider the idea that my physical existence is a decision made by my SS to help it fulfill what I will call the prime directive from AS: to develop, create, and evolve as part of the absolute expansion.

(*Personal note*: Words like *create*, *evolve*, and *expansion* are limited human communications. I believe I can see and understand beyond the words but cannot articulate beyond them. Sorry, but that is the best I can offer.)

28

CHANGE

Question/thought: The power and necessity of change

In the 1990s, I occasionally wrote an email to my entire department I called "Points to Ponder by Dr. SLK." Sometimes they were about interesting, curious, and unexplained scientific facts. Other times they would raise some type of philosophical question, and sometimes they were just an observation the intrigued me. Most of my department found them either humorous or interesting, and if I failed to write such an email for a few months, they would ask when Dr. SLK would be online again.

One of DR. SLK's more philosophical emails was titled "Embracing Change." Most comments about a "Points to Ponder" email usually came within the first day or two after I sent it. About eighteen months after the embracing change email was sent out, a lovely young lady who worked in the marketing department came into my office with a hard copy of my email and asked if I had written it. She went on to share that she was having some serious personal issues and had found a copy of the email and that it had been of great help to her in dealing with the pain she felt watching her father go through the dying process. I had written Points to Ponder primarily to show that research directors had a sense of whimsy in addition to our normally expressed serious persona. I was very surprised and honored that something of true benefit had come from Points to Ponder long after its distribution.

Twenty years after Points to Ponder went away, I was sipping my normal pre-lunch glass of beer when I realized (remembered) that I did not care for change. As I reflected on the Embracing Change Points to Ponder email, I started to think about the power of change—all types of change.

Change can generate intensely powerful feelings. Change can produce excitement, pain, happiness, fear, and so forth. Change can be viewed as a gain where we get something, an exchange where we lose something but get something to replace it, or entirely as a loss. Regardless, change always produces a reconfiguration of our energies. As we learn to deal with change (gain, exchange, and lose) that new energy melds with our previous energies and we grow and become more.

We can consider change to be positive, neutral, or negative. Regardless, change induces growth. Growth would not occur without change. In one view change can be viewed as always good since it gives us the opportunity for growth even if we would not choose it. It is most likely impossible to view the loss of a loved one, a job, or a relationship or developing a fatal disease as being potentially positive. But we can view something as painful as death as a reward for the departed, particularly if we believe in a pleasant Spirit Realm. They have completed their physical experience and are going home where we might meet them in our future.

A friend of mine was debating whether to go to a social event or not. A second friend said it did not really matter, stating that if she went, she would learn something, and if she stayed at home, she would learn something. Change can be viewed in a similar fashion. We can embrace it, numb ourselves to it, or deny it. Eventually we will learn from it. If we learn to face it and deal with it, we will progress faster and more easily than if we resist it. When we work with change, we can expand it, redirect it, or reverse the energy. No matter how we choose to deal with change, we will grow from the experience.

29

Beliefs I Am Unaware Of

Question/thought: Do I possess unrecognized belief systems?

During my usual morning spiritual rituals, my guide(s) raised a question for me to think about. The question was: Do you (Stan) accept beliefs and views without realizing you do so?

As I stated earlier in this book, I want to think, analyze, contemplate, and challenge everything before I accept any view that I am exposed to. I want to think for myself and not accept something as true just because someone else said it is so. I encourage others to do the same. I thought I was good at doing this, so the question somewhat surprised me.

I enjoy being exposed to different types of spiritual thought and thinkers. A few years ago, I spent several months studying the works of the Armenian mystic philosopher George Gurdjieff. It was his belief the people are so unconsciously programed by cultural habit that they have lost much of their free will and respond hypnotically to most things. I saw some validity in this view. Until the last fifty years, people were much like their parents. There was a uniformity in many communities and within various section of larger cities. While I have been very aware of the surface layer of my thinking processes as I looked deeper into my own behaviors and responses, I found that I have carried for much of my life many views that were not true or beneficial. After a few months of looking into my automatic response mechanisms and making corrections where needed, I moved on to new and richer experiences.

Because of my guide's question, I revisited this mind-mining process. My first thought was about my deteriorating health. Was I developing health issues solely because of the pathology associated with having lived nearly sixty years with diabetes, or did my thinking about being an old diabetic create at least some of my issues? I have heard motivational speakers say things like "We get what we expect," "We are what we believe we are," and "change your thinking and your life will change." My thoughts next went to the teachings on fear and how fear can attract to us that which we fear. I had lived my life up to retirement not really thinking I was a diabetic and was in very good health. The four-times-a-day insulin injections were just part of my daily routine, and my hypoglycemic events were just an opportunity to enjoy a candy bar. After my first retinal hemorrhage, that all changed, and I became fearful of additional retinal bleeds, which did rapidly occur. When my infected toe would not heal, I again became more fearful. I used to characterize that type of thinking as energizing my negativities. What is happening to me is typical, but I now question how much my subconscious beliefs that something will happen soon contributed to its manifestation.

My father was one of six foremen in his division. Over a ten period all of them except my dad suffered heart attacks. I could see my dad focusing on the thought that he too would experience a cardiac event. Several people close to him saw the same thing and cautioned him about his fearful thoughts. Two days after he retired, my father suffered his heart attack. I have no doubts that his fearful expectation significantly contributed to his heart issues.

I do not believe most health issues occur because we accept the view that at various points in our lives, certain illnesses are expected, but I do believe that blind acceptance of the inevitability of things happening to us plays a significant role in attracting those events. I think most people accept that there is some truth in the power of positive thinking. I also believe that there is power in negative thinking and sometimes those negative thoughts are so deeply buried in our minds that we do not realize we are holding them.

I can think of many valuable lessons I might be now learning. For instance, I have always viewed myself as a person who took care (at least financially) of others, but now I am learning to accept care being given to me. This is difficult for me. I also believe my guides were advising me to look deeply at the reason I respond as I do to accepting care and perhaps change my image of myself.

Part 4

30

A Brief Overview of My Life

I believe that our past, our life experiences, our culture, our age, and (for me) our health colors how we view, interpret, and articulate events. I am including this brief overview of my life so you might better understand the biases I have even though I personally do not recognize them. This might help you interpret what has been presented in parts 2 and 3. Part 4 is about me and not my guides' communications, so it's relatively unimportant and can be skipped.

Ages Zero to Five | 1945–1950

As I recall, I had an uneventful first five years of life. My father (my best friend for the first eighteen years of my life) worked very hard to support our family. He and I had little time to interact during the week, but on weekends we often went for walks in the woods around our home. I greatly enjoyed our weekend times together. Dad was the nurturer in my family while Mother provided most of the discipline. Dad was calm, kind, and very caring. His early life was very hard for him. An injury when he was thirteen almost killed him, and he was confined to bed for almost a year. He remained somewhat sickly throughout his teenage years. Dad tried very hard to be a good father, and while making some very apparent mistakes, he did an excellent job. He was my role model, and later in my life I realized he also was my hero. He never tried to stand out or to be noticed, but he worked very hard, albeit behind the scenes, to help others. Everyone loved my father.

My mother, father, and I always ate dinner together. My mother was completely in charge of the home: cooking, cleaning, laundry, and *me*. Since there were no other children close to my age in my community, I played mostly by myself, but I do not remember being bothered by being alone. My mother was always nearby but busy doing her housewife chores. I was always required to put my toys away when I was done playing with them. I became a very tidy and orderly child. I had a good imagination and could entertain myself without the involvement of others. Mom was also the driving force behind the family's religious activities.

Now it sounds odd, but I do remember having "spirit like" friends who appeared as spheres of various shades of light. They were about the size of a half dollar. When I was outside playing either in my yard or in the fields that surrounded our house, I would chase them trying to catch one. Whenever I got close, they would disappear and immediately reappear a few yards ahead of me. Several times I borrowed my father's fishing net to see if that would help. I never caught one. They were not physical. Initially my mother and other community members who observed me thought I was chasing butterflies that were quite plentiful where I lived. When winter came, there were no butterflies, and Mom asked me what I was chasing. When I told her, she said they were just my imagination and were not real. I was advised to stop chasing things that were not there or people would think I was crazy. For a few weeks after that conversation my sphere of light friends would appear, but I never tried to play with them. After that they never returned. Years later when I realized there was a spirit level, I recognized what they really were, wonderful spirit playmates for a little boy who was all alone. Or maybe Mom was right, but I do not think so.

Ages Six to Ten | 1951–1955

I entered first grade at the age of five years and seven months. If I had been born one day later (February 1), I would not have been allowed to go to school when I did but would have had to wait a year. In my school district, my parents had the option of enrolling me or to wait until the following year. Since I was large for my age, they decided I should start school. I was always the youngest student in my class and found the first half of the school year relatively difficult.

For the first three years of my schooling, I attended a small country school where all twelve grades (one through twelve) were housed in a small two-story brick building with six rooms on each level. First grade through sixth grade were on the ground floor and seventh through twelfth on the second level.

We were all country kids from the same socioeconomic class. That changed when I entered fourth grade since several local schools merged. My school and the school of a nearby city were united. At that point, over half my new class were kids from the city (actually a small town), and most of us country kids felt inferior and were treated that way by the classier and more wealthy townies. This was my first real experience of "them and us." A special writing teacher now came twice a week to instruct us in cursive writing. He was a very large and intimidating, no-nonsense man who I found very scary. I was the only left-handed student in the entire school, and the way the writing teacher made us hold the ink pen did not work for me. Rather than pulling the straight ink pen across the paper as the righties did, I had to push it, and the tip would catch on the paper, splattering ink over the paper, my desk, and me. My poor penmanship angered the teacher. He called me worthless and said I would be better off in the county jail than in his class. I thought I had ignored his outburst, but since I remember it from sixty-five years ago, I guess that is not so.

My younger brother was born while I was in first grade. My parents told me I was expected to help with my baby brother. I did not think much about that until I was twelve and my brother six. I decided I should help him develop as an athlete (baseball). My brother had a different idea. I was always super serious and responsible. My brother always thought life should be fun, so hard training was not in his playbook. He had a wild sense of humor and became the class cut up through high school and college. Neither of us ever became really good athletes, but he had a lot more fun and many more friends. Today I would say he is my best friend even though we live five hundred miles apart.

Ages Eleven to Fifteen | 1956–1960

As a seventh grader, I started attending the relatively large consolidated high school. As always, I remained a very average C student. Attending the "big" school was intimidating, and I felt very alone and out of place. In seventh grade I went out for the junior-high basketball team (seventh and eighth grades). While I was big for my age, I was not a good player. I did make the team, but that was about all. I do not remember playing in any games. During the summer between eighth and ninth grades, I worked very hard at basketball in the hope of making the junior varsity team (grades nine and ten). I was selected for the team and played some but never started a game. Early in the fall of my sophomore year, my weight suddenly dropped from 165 pounds to 119. I had developed type one insulin-dependent juvenile diabetes. I was hospitalized for almost a month to be regulated on insulin. In the hospital, I learned how to give myself daily injections and adapted to a very low-calorie diet. My parents kept me home from school for another seven or eight weeks until I regained some strength. Upon returning to school, I immediately went out for the JV basketball team. Although I made the team, I was too light and weak to enjoy playing basketball. Academically, it was difficult to make up all the school work I had missed.

Despite taking daily insulin injections, I was still on a very strict diet and was one of the few students who carried their lunch from home rather than eating the cafeteria-prepared food that contained more calories than I was allowed. This made me feel even more different and isolated.

The most difficult thing I had to accept after developing diabetes was that I now had no hope of going to the US Air Force Academy and becoming a fighter pilot (this had been my lifelong dream up to that point). My grades were probably not good enough to qualify for the academy (my color blindness and dyslexia would have also disqualified me, but I did not realize I had those issues at the time). Before developing diabetes, I had always loved airplanes and had dreamed of being an air force pilot. After developing diabetes, I was ultra-skinny and had few friends and no dreams. It was very depressing. While developing diabetes felt like the worst thing that had ever happened to me, it was actually a cruel blessing. I was very pro-military and undoubtedly would have gone to Vietnam a few years later if I had been allowed. Diabetes disqualified me from military service. Several of my high school classmates were killed in that war. I could have easily joined them had I been allowed to serve. Learning to cope with and in a way, overcome diabetes also helped/caused me to learn to deal with life in general and work through various setbacks.

Ages Sixteen to Twenty | 1961–1965

This was an event-filled half-decade. Early in my junior year, I decided not to be negatively impacted by my diabetes and began to exercise hard. I ran over five miles a day and lifted weights. I also decided, much to my parents' chagrin, to eat a more normal diet. Even when I adhered to a very strict diet, it proved very difficult (impossible) to control my diabetes. My blood glucose was usually too high, but I also had four to seven hypoglycemic events every week. I thought I would die young regardless of how I lived my life, so I tried to pack as much normalcy into however many years I had as I possibly could. Also, I had become very interested in girls and did not want to appear different or sickly. I became an acceptable varsity baseball and basketball player in my junior and senior years and enjoyed finishing my time in high school. I dated a few different girls and end up going steady (which meant exchanging class rings) with a very cute young lady who was first runner up for prom queen our senior year. That relationship ended when we went off to different colleges.

Due to having diabetes, I received a state-sponsored rehabilitation fellowship to continue my education and enrolled in a local college. I was able to live at home and commute to college, so the fellowship covered most of my expenses. My first three semesters were, as usual, average with me receiving one D, one B, and thirteen Cs. Then something happened, and I made the dean's list my fourth semester and every semester after that. I ended up graduating with honors. I had gone from being average to excelling. I have no Idea what happened. Maybe I started to work harder or smarter, or maybe I just matured. Whatever the reason, I am grateful.

Ages Twenty-One to Twenty-Five | 1966–1970

The next five years were also very eventful. I graduated from college (AB in chemistry) and decided to attend graduate school to pursue a PhD in organic chemistry. I applied to ten different graduate programs, and because of a relatively impressive undergraduate record and some very positive letters of recommendation, I was accepted to nine of them with the guarantee of either a teaching assistantship or a full fellowship at each. Either the teaching assistantship or the fellowship would cover all tuition costs and provide a small stipend to live on. I elected to go to Kent State University in Kent, Ohio, because it was within 150 miles from the community my then girlfriend and I had grown up in. I also chose Kent because they offered the most money—a full NASA fellowship paying $3,200 per year. My girlfriend and I decided to get married and move to Ohio. I felt very unprepared for graduate school and again, very out of place. Most of the other incoming graduate students were from better schools, and I did not know if I could compete with them or not. Despite this I did fairly well my first year, earning a 3.2 GPA in my coursework. I selected a thesis advisor my first summer and start my PhD research project. I worked very long hours (8:00 a.m. to 9:00 or 9:30 p.m. six and a half days a week). My research went well, but my marriage did not. It seemed I was good at research but not so good with relationships. That would often repeat itself throughout my life. I quickly published my first scientific paper, which pleased me and made my parents proud. They could now say they had a published son.

Soon after this, I had a near-death/out-of-body experience. This was a pivotal experience in my life. My wife and I had dated a little in high school but never seriously. We went to the same church and so saw each other regularly. During my second year in college and her first year in nursing school, we became more serious and got married shortly after we each graduated in 1966. We were both twenty-one, and neither of us were prepared for marriage. We had difficulties from the start, and six months after my NDE, my wife and I separated. We were in the process of getting a divorce when she was killed in an early morning traffic accident. She appeared to me in what seemed like a very real dream at the moment she died. I immediately woke up with a profound feeling of loss and loneliness. I could not go back to sleep and so went to my lab. At around nine o'clock I was called to the department chairman's office, where a state trooper informed me of her death. I went completely numb, left the lab, called my parents, and walked around town in the rain for the next six hours.

Later that afternoon my parents arrived after driving the 150 miles between their home to where I lived to see if I was okay and to take me back to their community where my wife would be buried. The numbness left and was replaced by sadness and guilt. I felt responsible for my wife's death, although I was not directly involved. I felt I had been a poor husband and if I had been a better partner, we would not have separated and she would not have been killed. Facing her friends and family was very difficult even though her family was very loving and caring toward me. After three weeks, I returned to my lab to finish my research, which led to three more publications. I was in the middle of writing my formal thesis when May 4, 1970, occurred. Four students were killed at Kent State, and several others were wounded when the Ohio National Guard (which had been called to the campus because of student demonstrations against the war in Vietnam) indiscriminately opened fire on various groups of students. The death of my wife, followed by these senseless killings, really changed me. I had always been a very conservative, pro-military person. Overnight I became very liberal, anti-war, and more socially involved. Over the years since Kent State, I have become even more liberal as my consciousness evolved and I had more life experiences.

Ages Twenty-Six to Thirty | 1971–1975

By the fall of 1970 I had started casually dating. My thesis had been accepted, and I was awarded a PhD in chemistry. I accepted an offer to do postdoctoral research at the Ohio State University. Shortly after moving from Kent to Columbus, I met a striking, attractive young lady who would later become my second wife and the mother of my two children. We started dating, and after a year of being together, she just stopped going home. It was a very enjoyable and exciting time as we started to talk about what we should do with the rest of our lives. In graduate school,

I had focused on organic chemistry but found biochemistry much more interesting. We decided that I should consider obtaining a second PhD in biochemistry, during which time she could help support us. I wrote to several graduate schools in warmer parts of the United States so I could play tennis in my spare time and she could ride her horse.

Professor Earl Sutherland had just won the Nobel Prize in Medicine and Physiology. Dr. Sutherland was then at Vanderbilt University in Nashville, Tennessee. I was interested in his work, so I applied there. A few weeks later I received a 6:30 a.m. phone call (5:30 in Nashville) from Vanderbilt informing me that they would consider me for graduate school if I wanted, but perhaps it would be better for me to go to Vanderbilt as a postdoctoral fellow since I already had a PhD. If I did the latter, I would be allowed to audit any lectures that interested me, and I would be paid a significant salary working as a postdoctoral researcher. This appealed to both me and my then-girlfriend. Vanderbilt said they were impressed with my academic accomplishments but that I would still have to go through a formal interview to determine if I would fit into the high-powered research environment at Vandy. My girlfriend and I took a weekend road trip to Tennessee before the Tuesday interview at Vanderbilt. We both walked from our hotel to the Physiology Department on Tuesday morning. I assumed that my interview would take an hour or so, and I wanted my girlfriend to be present because we would then make an informed joint decision if I was offered a position. We met with the head of recruitment, who informed us that my interview would last all day and then unceremoniously dismissed my girlfriend, sending her back to the hotel.

During the eight hours of interviews, I met with the entire department and the world-renowned department chairman, who was a friendly and brilliant person. The one thing I learned from my interviews was that most of the then-current department faculty in physiology initially entered the department as postdoctoral fellows of one type or another. It seemed that they did not offer postdoctoral positions to people unless a candidate seemed capable of competing for a full-time tenure-track faculty position. I thought my interviews went well and was very impressed with the faculty and environment but was unsure what would happen next.

My girlfriend and I then returned to Columbus. For some reason, I kept visualizing myself as a full-time faculty member at Vanderbilt. I did not do this intentionally, but that image keep coming into my mind as I walked to and from work or went for my daily run. This turned out to be one of my more successful manifestations through visualization practices. A few weeks later, I received an official offer to become a visiting investigator in Vanderbilt's Department of Physiology. I immediately accepted.

We again traveled to Nashville to find an apartment for us and a stable for my girlfriend's horse. The following week I resigned from my position at OSU, my girlfriend became my wife, and we had her horse transported to a lovely barn/farm just outside of Nashville. Three days later we were Tennessee residents. Almost everyone at the university was very friendly, and I started doing research in a very exciting area that I knew little about.

I worked very hard and learned quickly. Within a year, I published a paper on my work in a very prestigious scientific journal. My wife got a job as a dental hygienist and rode her horse almost every weekend while I worked in the lab on Saturday morning and played tennis Saturday afternoons and on Sunday. I also got involved with a running club (the Nashville Striders) and ran four to five miles every night after work. On Sunday morning, the club met for a longer run (six to eleven miles). Most every Friday and Saturday night my wife and I partied hard, being young and healthy and living in a very exciting city.

Ages Thirty-One to Thirty-Five | 1976–1980

Things went well for me professionally during this period. I was publishing two to four papers a year and became a tenure track faculty member at Vanderbilt. My first child was born, and I experienced the unconditional love a parent gives a child and how a child gives that love back to the parent. I started to grow tired of working sixty to seventy hours a week because this took time away from my young family. Also, my wife and I were slowly growing apart. It seemed like time with our daughter was one of the few enjoyments we shared. I decided that while I loved academic life, the insecurity of having to constantly struggle to obtain research monies from government sources was too much of a burden. Therefore, I started looking at academic appointments at less high-powered universities.

I also explored industrial research positions, which provided significantly more income. Soon I was offered a senior scientist position with McNeil Pharmaceuticals (a division of Johnson & Johnson). After much soul searching and discussions with my wife, I accepted this offer and moved with my family to a Philadelphia suburb. I enjoyed pharmaceutical research. It brought more money and more free time. J&J was a great company, dedicated to serving its customers and treating their employees honestly and fairly. While I only had three junior researchers reporting to me, I was sent to management school soon after I arrived. The purpose of this training was to cultivate an appreciation of the professional needs of everyone reporting me and to learn personnel-related problem solving. During my time with J&J, I learned what a well-managed organization looked like and how it functioned. I was sent to (or allowed to attend) several management and strategy planning courses while with McNeil. These helped me greatly as I moved up the managerial ladder. I was very fortunate to work for J&J. It taught me how and when to deal with issues and when to allow them time and space to organically dissolve. It reinforced my realization that people perform better when treated with respect rather than creating an atmosphere of fear and intimidation. I assumed this method of management was commonplace. I was quickly proven wrong.

Ages Thirty-Six to Forty-Five | 1981–1990

While I was happy and well respected at McNeil, I followed the money and was recruited away by another large pharmaceutical company. I was required to move to another state three months before my daughter's school year finished, so I commuted over two hundred miles each week between my work and Philadelphia. During this time, I was only able to see my family on weekends. In my opinion, although my new department was very successful, it was poorly managed, with a huge number of employee issues. Most of these went unaddressed or dismissed with a perspective like, "This is the way it is. Now go back to work." I did not like being away from my family. I did not like the new job. And I did not like being told by my boss that the best way to manage people was to create a sense of fear. And I did not like my new location.

After my family was able to join me, things improved. My second child was born a year later. He was a joy. My daughter was now a sparkling six-year-old, and while my wife was providing most of the care of our infant son, my daughter and I started spending a lot of quality time together. It was during this time that one of the most precious events of my life occurred. During the winter of 1983, I had started getting up around 5:30 and going jogging before work. One morning as I returned to my home, I saw a small object moving toward me. At first, I did not realize what it was, but as I got closer, I realized it was my seven-year-old daughter, who had gotten up on her own, put on her winter coat over her nightgown and her boots, and come out to join Dad for his jog. I do not think I have ever felt so loved by a physical being or more grateful as I did in that moment. Small acts can have monumental meaning.

While my family life was very enjoyable, things at work were not going well. A number of my fellow managers went to corporate in an attempt to do something about our boss. I was not one of them but would have supported their efforts if they had asked me. Looking back, I realize that my time at this second company did induce great growth. I had to address many different types of problems, and while it produced a lot of pain and anxiety, it demanded that I think outside the box. It showed me that while I was a shy introvert, I was an effective manager. I realized I had more talent dealing with people than with test tubes. Shortly thereafter I was very happy (and very frightened) to accept a position with my third big pharm company as director of preclinical cardiovascular research. Again, my family and I changed locations as I moved into a new position with much greater responsibility, more stress, and better pay. The new position demanded that I grow both as a person and as a leader.

Shortly after I moved into my new position, my father died. He had been fighting cancer for some time, but it was still quite a blow. He had always been there for me. I knew he was proud of me and that his spirit continues, but I still miss his physical presence. He did visit me the night before his burial to tell me he was okay and that he loved me. I have not had any additional visual visits but often feel his presence especially when I am golfing. He was an avid golfer.

Although we had two awesome children that both my wife and I cherished, we had grown far apart. After a year or so, we decided to separate. I continued to pay all the bills and had complete access to my children. I did not like being without my children every night but saw them almost every evening and on the weekends except when I was traveling for work.

When I took the position with my third company, I knew that within a few years they planned to consolidate all their research activities in another state. As this time grew closer, my wife and I decided to try living together again and to move as a family to where I was being transferred. This attempt at reconciliation was very stressful. We both still held much unresolved anger and disappointment. Also, during our separation I had started dating a lady I knew from work. This greatly complicated things. I do not know if there are such things as soul mates, but if there are, we certainly could have been ones. We had very similar views toward most things, and our energies potentiated each other. While we were both very competent at work, our individual productivity (at least mine) dramatically increased when we were together. We were also both very interested in psychic phenomena, philosophy, and spirituality. Regardless of our attraction toward each other, we decided to end the relationship when my wife and I attempted to get our acts together.

Housing prices in the state I was required to move to were the highest in the continental United States at that time. This required people who were moving into that state to pay a lot more for a lot less in relationship to purchasing a home. After several days of looking at houses and arguing with each other, my wife had had enough and returned home to the Midwest. After a sleepless night of soul searching, my wife called to tell me she would not move with me and that she and the children were going back to Oklahoma, where she had grown up. I was devastated and became very depressed. While I did not really want to live with anyone, to have my kids a thousand miles away was absolutely awful. My depression deepened, and I started drinking a little too much. I was just going through the motions at work and did not contribute as much as I expected from myself. While we were not able to live together, my wife and I remained on good terms. I rented an apartment close to where my new laboratories were and bought a house in Tulsa for my wife and children. At work, I had a lot of responsibility and was paid well. My wife and I split my salary, and I put my bonuses in a savings account for the kids (cars when they turned sixteen and college when they were ready). I was able to travel from Hartford to Tulsa every third weekend to be with my children and spent a week at Thanksgiving and at Christmas with them. Although my wife and I were now estranged, she always welcomed me into her home when I traveled to see our children. Today we are still very good friends and talk often about our children and how each of us is doing.

My soul mate and I later reconnected. She had left the corporation we both worked for and started her own company. She did a lot of business with a number of major medical groups, universities, and pharmaceutical companies in the area of the country where I was living. This required her to travel a lot, and she often was able to visit me on the weekends when she was traveling to research sites close to where I lived. We both enjoyed reading books on nonordinary reality, metaphysics, spirituality, and philosophy. We enjoyed being together and exploring the spiritual part of being. It was unbelievable how our energies merged and expanded. She was perfectly attractive and very energetic and brought a wonderful new path to my life. I could not imagine a more perfect human. I still cannot understand why she agreed to hang with me. The immense pleasure, enjoyment, growth, and fun she brought into my life were equaled by the pain I experienced several years later when we ended our relationship. Oddly, that pain caused me to reassess my life up to that point and made me look within for validation. As thankful as I am that we magically came together, I am as grateful for the lessons I had to learn when we came apart, as painful as it was.

Because of the pain and guilt of my separation from my kids, I talked with a couple of local counselors and tried to ease my pain with lots of physical activity. This all helped, but I hated being so far away from my children as well as my soul mate. I had no attachment to staying where I was, so I wrote to over fifty science-based companies that were closer to Tulsa and my children. I also contacted several corporate headhunters (independent recruiters). Nothing much came from this effort for over a year. Then, in the same week, I was contacted by two major pharmaceutical companies. One was a major European company with US headquarters in New Jersey, and the other was the nutritional division of Abbott Laboratories (Ross Labs), which was located in Columbus, Ohio. I interviewed with both companies and got second interviews with both. I was asked to visit the European headquarters for the New Jersey company and got a very attractive offer from Abbott/Ross. I liked the people at Ross, it was a lot closer to Tulsa, and I knew and liked Columbus from my earlier experiences while at Ohio State. I gratefully accepted the Ross offer and became the director of strategic research, initially reporting to the VP of R&D.

Ages Forty-Six to Fifty-Five | 1991–2001

My job was now primarily managing research scientists, creating an environment where they could flourish, identifying new opportunities, and problem solving. I was pretty good at all these aspects. Things went relatively well for me, and I was rewarded with significant salary increases, bonuses, and stock options. I was closer to Oklahoma and got to see my children more often. I spoke to them almost every day. I was also nearer to where my soul mate lived, so we were able to get together more frequently. Both personally and professionally things went well for me during this period. After a few years at Ross, there was a major reorganization, and I got a new boss who was very proactive and great fun to work with. We are still good friends today.

Within a three-week period during the summer of 1996, I became aware of four parents who either worked in my department or were friends of mine all of who had a child diagnosed with ADHD (attention deficit hyperactivity disorder). As they individually told me what their kid had gone through and how much happier they now were after starting ADHD medication, I realized I had all the symptoms of a person with adult

ADHD. I saw a psychologist and was tested and retested for that disorder. At that time when an adult said they thought they had ADHD, there was concern they were just trying to get drugs (stimulants). One of the many tests I was subjected to was a multi-dimensional intelligence test. I had had several IQ tests throughout my life and had always scored between 130 and 135, which was high enough that I should not have had to struggle as much as I did at school and college. The MDIQ test measured my IQ in eight different areas. In the verbal/vocabulary/linguistic area I scored quite low. In logical reasoning, spatial relationships, and situational interpretation, my scores were very high. In the remaining areas that were tested, I was about average. This helped me understand why I was able to accomplish so much with relative ease in some areas and felt so dumb in others. Understanding what areas I was gifted in and what areas I was not gifted allowed me to select projects and situations I could handle well and what type of projects or activities I needed to avoid as much as possible.

Other tests showed that I did indeed have ADHD as well as dyslexia. I started taking Ritalin, and it was like a veil lifted. I was able to concentrate much better and had greatly improved interpersonal interactions. I could speak spontaneously rather than having to think about every word I was going to use before I spoke. I was also much happier with myself. Unfortunately, I passed the ADHD trait, as well as Gilbert's syndrome, on to my son. Fortunately, neither of my children inherited my diabetes, but both my kids and my grandson inherited the Keely super-large head (hat size 7.75). It is good that none of us like to wear hats.

It was around 1994 (give or take a year) that my son called to tell me that he was the first student from his class to be selected into the gifted program and that he would now be taking a high school algebra class with students two or three years his senior. My son was happy but did not attach great significance to this. However, he wanted to share his honor with me. I was unbelievably happy and very grateful that he chose to share it with me as soon as he got home from school. I had great guilt not being more involved with my children as they grew up. It eases my pain to see them do so very well and be so loving. Many "that a girl" to their mother for doing such a great job.

Things between me and my soul mate were changing, and shortly after the turn of the century, she gave me an ultimatum that I could not agree to and we ended our relationship. Maybe there is no such thing as soul mates or maybe soul mates are not supposed to be together for any longer than we were. Regardless, it was very painful for both of us. I think our coming together stimulated each other's spiritual growth and evolution. For me the breakup, painful as it was, drove me to even greater inquiry into the spiritual forces all around us. The greater spiritual growth that came later would not have happened if I had not had the relationship and experienced its ending.

Ages Fifty-Six to Sixty-Five | 2001–2010

Without a doubt, I went through the five stages of grief when my soul mate-like relationship dissolved. Eventually I started casually dating a couple of women from work but was not interested in any type of significant involvement. After seven or eight months, I had accepted the breakup but was still quite wounded. In an effort to heal, I started therapy sessions with a holistic coach and medical intuitive. I did a number of one-on-one sessions and started to do three-day-weekend training seminars (ten to twelve hours each day) to learn how to be a holistic coach myself. Essentially all the people attending the three-day seminars were doing so because they had experienced some type of life trauma and wanted to address and heal these painful personal issues. There were anywhere from twenty to fifty individuals per seminar, and we practiced holistic coaching on each other. Usually we were very supportive of each other, and the training proved extremely valuable to me. In my third training seminar, the instructor selected me to come in front of the group as an example of a person who had experienced much loss in their life. He intuitively knew that I had a number of distant losses in addition to the loss of my soul mate. The purpose was to demonstrate to the group how holistic coaching could be used to heal the pain experienced from loss. I assumed he would process me through some unresolved issues I had not addressed about my first wife and her death, which I still felt responsible for, or about not being more available to loved ones, particularly my two children. The instructor used a technique called kinesiology muscle testing to guide him in identifying issues that the subject was hiding or was unaware of. I volunteered that I would guess the most significant unhealed loss I had experienced was the death of my first wife. The testing indicated that this was not the case, and after a couple more muscle tests, the instructor determined my most significant unhealed loss had occurred when I was about five years old. Immediately the memory of the old farmer (Bill) who lived on the other side of the blacktop country road that ran by my house returned to me. He had been like a second father or grandfather to me. In 1950, he still worked his fields with horse-drawn farm equipment. He drove a horse and wagon to the local grocery store when he needed food or other supplies. I would walk behind him as he plowed his fields, looking for arrowheads in the turned over soil. He taught me to husk corn and churn butter. I was telling the group how very wonderful this old farmer was to me and that I often drank buttermilk with him even though I hated its taste. I felt this was quite funny and was smiling as I shared it with the group, but when I said, "Even though I hated its taste," my smile suddenly turned into a flood of tears. The day Bill died, I had walked over to his house to see what we were going to do that day. I found him leaning against the porch of his old farmhouse, unable to speak. His grandson had arrived just before I did and was running to get help. I had no Idea what was happening. Later that morning my second dad died. That was my first experience with death and loss. I had never cried for my dear old friend, but I unashamedly made up for it that day in front of the group. A scab had been torn off my soul, and that night I started processing all of my losses that I had not realized I had. I had completely numbed out a large number of tragic losses because "boys were not supposed to cry," and I had shut down a good deal of my ability to feel. I had lost much of my ability to feel pain but also much of my ability to experience positive feelings like love, happiness, joy, etc. Unfortunately, I had not shut down my ability to feel anger, jealousy, and fear. Up until that time, I had been living a very unbalanced life. I believe (because of my NDE) that my dear friend is still very much alive in the spirit realm and expect him and my actual father to meet me when I transition.

I had been viewed as a strong, stoic intellectual person by my weekend groups until my meltdown. I was still seen somewhat that way but now viewed as a warmer and more approachable person. Shortly after my meltdown, an attractive lady somewhat my junior who was also attending the seminar came up to me as we were breaking for lunch and asked if she could buy me the meal. She said it looked to her as if I need "looking after" for a while after my emotional release. Over the next few months, we found ourselves in the same weekend workshop several times. We both were very interested in spirituality, metaphysics, nonordinary reality, hypnosis, and holistic coaching. We start dating and soon became exclusive. While we never officially moved in together, we considered ourselves life partners.

Thanks to ten years of stock options (part of my performance bonus), I was able to retire from corporate life, and my new partner and I started the holistic coaching company called Transpersonal Life Development. I had just turned fifty-seven when this new part of my life started. During our time together, we traveled to many different spiritual centers, studying and experiencing several different consciousness perspectives. These included Shambhala Buddhism, Shamanism, cranial-sacral therapy, heart-centered therapy, and clinical hypnosis, among others.

We thought we would help a lot of people and perhaps become rich and famous in the process. By the end of our first year, we were helping a significant number of clients and teaching classes on alternative medicine, but we started having strong disagreements over how to conduct our business activities and realized we did not have enough clients for two people. We worked less and less as a team and more as individual coaches. We decided to dissolve the business partnership. We remained life partners for another year, and then that ended too. We remain friends today and occasionally talk on the phone. Again, I believe the time we were together was extremely beneficial to both of us as we experienced a number of intense spiritual adventures. Although we were no longer a couple, we both deepened our study of Shambhala Buddhism. We attended a dathun (a four-week meditation retreat) together and Sutrayana Seminary and Vajrayana Seminary separately. She continues to study Shambhala Buddhism. I am still very interested in Buddhism and continue to use many of the meditation practices I learned from that path.

Spiritually, I now tell people I am a "Stan-ist." This is my attempt to convey I have my own individual spiritual path and philosophy, which incorporates many of the views and practices I learned from Christianity, Buddhism, Shamanism, Taoism, and the Kabbalah, as well as my personal insights.

In the spring of 2003, I noticed blood in my urine after a strenuous tennis match. This continued to occur each time I exercised. I saw my primary care physician, and he had me undergo an ultrasound evaluation. The ultrasound showed a small kidney stone in my right kidney and a much larger stone in my left kidney. I previously had several kidney stones and underwent procedures known as ultrasound lithotripsy, which uses sound waves to break up the kidney stones into a fine, gravel-like material that can be excreted in the urine. My PCP had me go to a urologist, who immediately scheduled a lithotripsy for me. I had a bad reaction to the anesthesia used during the procedure and had to have support breathing for a few hours following the lithotripsy. After recovery, I noticed there was much less gravel in my urine than I expected, and I continued to have significant pain for the next several days, which had not been the case with my previous procedures. Because of my pain, I saw my surgeon who, after an X-ray, told me that although he had blasted the stone out of my left kidney, he had failed to break it up, and it was now lodged in my ureter, blocking urine flow from the kidney to the bladder. He wanted to do another lithotripsy, but I had no faith in his medical skills and saw a second physician to get another opinion. By the time I saw the second physician, my ureter had become very infected and I was starting to become septic. The second doctor told me that the stone was so close to my descending aorta that lithotripsy would have a very significant chance of rupturing that blood vessel. He immediately scheduled surgery to use a medical laser to break up the stone. It proved impossible to get the laser through my ureter to the stone because of the infection. He was able to insert a stint around the infected tissue, which allowed urine flow to be reestablished and greatly lessened my pain. I went on a four-week antibiotic regimen, after which time he was able to insert the medical laser and break up the stone, which was then excreted in my first urination following this third surgery.

After the failed lithotripsy, as the infection developed, I became very ill and barely had enough energy to get out of bed. As I laid in bed, I could feel the life force go out of my body. This was a very unpleasant experience. During this time, I lost the ability to sleep, and all I did was to lay in bed and reflect on my life. Although I did not realize it at the time, I believe my spirit guides helped as I reviewed my life up to that point. I found that I had two major regrets. The first was that I had not been as emotionally available to my loved ones as I could have been and wished I had. The second regret was that I had not pursued my spiritual path with as much vigor as I could have. As soon as I recovered from the botched lithotripsy, which had almost killed me, I traveled to see as many of my past and current loved ones as I could, apologizing for being as distant as I had been. Since then I have always attempted to be as supportive and involved as possible. I also became completely dedicated to my spiritual pursuits. Both activities proved to be very valuable and rewarding.

Ages Sixty-Six to Seventy-Two | 2011–2017

After several years without any interaction, my soul mate from eight years earlier sent me an email saying she had "come full circle" and had accepted a position at Vanderbilt University. We both had worked at Vandy during the '70s but did not know each other at that time. Since my daughter and her family were living in Nashville, my former soul mate invited me to stop by and have a glass of wine sometime when I was visiting my daughter. It was about ten months before our schedules overlapped—me visiting my daughter and her having open time. She had a large house, so it was agreed that I would come to Nashville a day early, stay at her house that night, and play a round of golf the next day before going to my daughter's house for the rest of my week visit. When she opened the door, it was as if we had never been apart. We both had markedly changed. Her hair was much shorter, my hair was gone, and my dark beard was now gray. But there was still a deep knowing. We spent that evening talking about what had happened to each of us over the past decade and where we were at in life. Even though we had grown in different directions (I had become much more liberal, independent, and secular, while she was now very conservative, republican, and even more religious than she had been before), there was still great appreciation of each other. We got together again two months later (wine and golf) and decided that we would start seeing each other as much as we could even though I was living in Columbus, Ohio, and she was living In Tennessee.

I had lived with diabetes for over forty years without any major problems even with my fast and hard-driving lifestyle. Shortly after the turn of the century, I started to have retinal bleeds due to proliferative retinopathy. I required several laser treatments and two invasive eye surgeries to deal with this. At the fifty-year-mark of my diabetes (I was sixty-four), I developed a severe foot ulcer that did not respond to treatment. It would require femoral artery angioplasty followed by major foot surgery. Also, I developed a hole in my right retina as my foot problem was being addressed, and this required another eye surgery. A couple friends from the Columbus Shambhala group, my brother, and my son took time out of their lives to help me get to and from the hospitals for my various surgeries. My old now-new significant other/soul mate, who was now the executive director of a major research program at Vanderbilt, keep taking vacation time to travel from Nashville to Columbus to be with me as I dealt with my health issues. One time her 4:00 p.m. flight to Columbus was canceled due to severe snow, and she and her daughter rented a car and drove four hundred miles through the night on snow-covered roads, arriving in Columbus a few minutes before I had to leave for my 5:15 a.m. report time for 7:00 a.m. foot surgery.

A few weeks earlier my son-in-law had asked me if I would ever consider moving to Tennessee since my grandson, who was seven, my daughter, he, and now my significant other/soul mate were all there. I had thought I might move sometime after my son graduated from the Ohio State Medical School, where he was a third-year medical student, but my health was deteriorating so rapidly and all the trips between Nashville and Columbus were requiring a lot of my soul mate's time and energy (although she never complained), so I decided I would look at Tennessee properties the next time I visited there. I contacted a realtor from Nashville, and over the next three weeks she sent me over 250 property listings that were in my price range. I selected thirty-six listings I wanted to look at, thinking it would take at least four trips to Tennessee to see all thirty-six houses. We selected eight houses I wanted to look at on my first day of house hunting. When I walked into the second house we were scheduled to see that first day, the energy was very strong, with a very high vibration. My soul mate and I looked through the house without sharing our thoughts or feelings. After we completed our first inspection, we shared our impressions and opinions. We had both felt the same high energy. We visited three more houses before I told the realtor I did not want to look at any more properties that day but would like to go back to that second house. While there was some furniture and dishes in the house, there was no one living there, so a second visit that day was easily accommodated. This time the next-door neighbors came over and after introducing themselves, told us about life in the community. The next day the realtor and I visited the property a third time, after which I told her I wanted to make an offer I thought was fair even though it was lower than the listing price. Two days later the owners accepted my offer and asked if I could close early since they had a significant mortgage they wanted to pay off. They had already moved out of state. What I thought was going to be a six-month effort was completed in less than a week with closing two weeks later. My soul mate and I did a walkthrough the day before closing and just happened to run into the owners, who were removing the show furniture. They were a wonderful couple who had loved the property but were very happy to be able to pay off their mortgage. They were kind enough to go through the house with us and showed me how everything worked. The buying and selling of this high-energy house was definitely a win/win. Everything just fell into place. It showed me that when something is supposed to happen, it can happen quickly and with ease. I liked Columbus and did not want to leave until after my son had graduated, but this felt like what I was supposed to do.

Now

That was seven years ago. My home is now my sanctuary. It's open and bright. I converted the small third bedroom into a shrine room, where I meditate and conduct various spiritual practices. I have a large leather captain's chair that looks out onto the wooded backyard, where I read as I have my morning coffee. My soul mate has moved twice since I have been here and now lives about ten miles away. Despite not being in the best health, we usually have dinner together several times a week and spend part of each weekend together unless one of us is doing something with our respective grandchildren. She has four and I have one.

My son graduated from medical school, completed a three-year pediatric residency program in Milwaukee, and fifteen months ago moved to Nashville. He arrived here just as I started having issues with my toes due to compromised microvascular circulation, a byproduct of fifty-eight years of diabetes. Over the past year I have had two more femoral artery angioplasties and four toe surgeries, losing three toes in total. Between my soul mate, son, and daughter, I have had great, loving care. I am very blessed to have the helpers and caregivers I do.

I hope I am through with hospitals and that I will peacefully move into the light while resting or sleeping in my blessed home. If that is not what happens, I hope I have the courage, strength, and insight to see what I am learning from whatever comes my way.

Part 5

31

My Current Core Beliefs

There is no reason anyone should care what my current core beliefs are. Most assuredly they are not fixed and will change as my consciousness evolves. I include them here for the sake of transparency.

1. I firmly believe in a nonphysical existence that is eternal. This is primarily due to my ND/OBE.
2. I believe in evolution and that there are several forms of evolution. I believe that within every form or formless existence there is an intelligence and drive that can bring about its own evolution and growth into a more complex and capable presence.
3. I believe we are spiritual beings that never cease and continue to develop and grow beyond time and space.
4. I believe there is an uncaused cause (UCC) that is responsible for everything. The UCC is beyond human ability to conceptualize or to know. I refer to it as Absolute Source.
5. I believe Absolute Source either is or created the drive to grow and evolve and gave everything a primordial intelligence and free will. Beyond that, I do not believe Absolute Source is involved with the progression or growth of anything. That is up to the evolving presence, which is self-responsible.
6. I believe that thoughts and visualizations, which are spirit in nature, can manifest into the physical realm. Although the current ability to physically manifest is poorly developed, this is an area of future evolution.

The End

0416O8O6-009557 97

Printed in the United States
By Bookmasters